Facing Federer

Symposium of a Champion

By Scoop Malinowski

(Copyright 2013 Mark Scoop Malinowski)

ACKNOWLEDGEMENTS

In two decades covering professional sport, I have gathered a lot of miscellaneous information and anecdotes about Roger Federer, many of which reveal a more personal essence of his character, outside of what we see in the tennis arena and media realm. There was enough material, I hoped, to compile, arrange and produce into a very entertaining and informative book.

In the embryonic stages, this project originally aspired to be, not a normal, conventional book but an abstract portrait and symposium about the great champion Roger Federer, a collection of interviews, perspectives, memories, photos and art work. However, as we know, plans do often go awry and this creation unexpectedly evolved into a different direction. At the 2012 U.S. Open, as an experiment, I interviewed several ATP players about their matches against Roger Federer and was pleasantly thrilled by their engaging cooperation in sharing special accounts and details about actual duels with the living legend.

After more interviews with Pete Sampras, Andre Agassi, Patrick Rafter, Jim Courier and John McEnroe at a senior exhibition at Madison Square Garden in New York City in late 2012, I decided to attend the Delray Beach International Tennis Championships in February, the Masters Series Sony Open in Miami in March, and the Sarasota Open Challenger in Longboat Key, Florida in April to attempt to interview as many players as possible who have competed against or practiced with Federer. I'm very happy to say the mission was a complete success and over 50 players graciously discussed their experiences on court and off with Federer.

So the project has metamorphosed into this new, final form...with the "Facing Federer" aspect as the primary nucleus.

To gain access and cooperation to tackle such a project like this required a lot of help, patience and thoughtfulness from so many different people and organizations. Even the one ATP player who declined to talk about his experiences with Federer on court could not have been nicer about it. He said Roger was not happy about a previous book written about him and he specifically asked this friend to please decline any interview requests about him as a book subject.

All the other players were wonderfully cooperative. So many people associated with the sport were very helpful, including: Patrick Rafter, Attila Savolt, Tommy Haas, Nicola Arzani, Gilles Muller, Andrei Pavel, Jim Courier, James Blake, Boris Sobkin, Rainer Schuettler, Jan-Michael Gambill, Mark Knowles, Somdev Devvarman, Pete Sampras, Andre Agassi, Alejandro Falla, Cedrik-Marcel Stebe, Ilija Bozoljac, Yen-Hsun Lu, Tomas Berdych, Nathan Healey, Rick Leach, Dmitry Tursunov, Steve Johnson, Paul Capdeville, Alex Dolgopolov, Denis Istomin, Xavier Malisse, Arnaud Clement, Sebastien Grosjean, Dominik Hrbaty, Teymuraz Gabashvili, Peter Luczak, Alex Bogomolov Jr., Brad Falkner, Sania Mirza, Marion Bartoli, Tracy Singian, Lisa Franson, Anne Marie McLaughlin, IMG's Gary Swain, Sam Henderson and Kayla Holst.

Many other colleagues and associates in the media business were also helpful with their suggestions, ideas and enthusiasm: Dan Markowitz, Richard Pagliaro, Dan C. Weil, Rob Koenig, Greg Sharko, Harry Cicma, Vivienne Christie, Maylene Ramey, Christian Koskorelos to name a few. Also special thanks to Earnest Joseph for his technical assistance and ASAP Sports for providing press conference transcripts.

Table Of Contents - Chapters

Chapter 1: "The God Of Tennis"

A lot of people have been awed by the achievements and actions of Roger Federer...

Henri Leconte (Former ATP Player): "I like to watch Federer, of course. Because he can do whatever he wants."

Akiko Morigami (Former WTA Player): "I think he's like the God of tennis."

Lleyton Hewitt (ATP Player): "Roger's Roger. He's the greatest player of all time."

Wladimir Klitschko (World Heavyweight champion): "Roger Federer, he's the champion. Tennis is a great sport. And if you meet, personally, those big guys like Roger Federer, you're just so inspired, and following and looking at it. And it's amazing that he just keeps on winning and keeps winning, which is not common in sport. I met him personally two years ago in Germany at an awards gala. He's very handsome and very, very down to earth guy. And I think as a person, he's not complicated. And just a real nice person. And he told me he's a Klitschko fan, he watched my fights of me and my brother. He said he definitely wants to come to the fights."

Heidi Albertsen (Supermodel): "It was my birthday on September 1 some years ago. I was at the U.S. Open during a day session, as some friends of mine were playing that day. I was sitting in the stands with two Swiss players that day who are friends with Roger Federer. They invited me to stay to the evening session to watch Roger play in the semifinals. Of course I agreed. How could I say no? We watched the semifinals and were seated in the players' box, the section reserved for their families, trainers, and friends, and I was seated next to his then girlfriend and now wife Miroslava Vavrinec. I felt so fortunate to have been at the right time and right place, as it was an incredible experience. He played extremely well and won that match. Miroslava has a thoughtful and caring personality -- one that completely lacks pretense. She invited me afterwards to have dinner with Roger and his trainers. We dined inside at the restaurant at Arthur Ashe Stadium that is reserved for the players. Kenneth Carlsen, a Danish professional tennis player, along with his wife, were dining at a table next to our's. All of us had a nice conversation over dinner. I can say without a doubt that Roger and Miroslava are among the nicest and most genuine people who I've ever encountered in my lifetime. Roger has a great personality and is as poised at the dinner table as he is on the tennis court. He is well-mannered and well-spoken, interesting and humorous. Miroslava is amazingly sweet, and the two of them compliment each other beautifully. It was a birthday I will always treasure."

John McEnroe (Former ATP Player): "Federer plays tennis the way I dreamed of playing. He could be the most talented player I've ever seen, someone who comes along only every 10 or 20 years. If you want to be a tennis player, then mold yourself on Roger Federer. I won three Wimbledon titles and I wish I could play like him."

Tracy Austin (Former WTA Player): "I've never enjoyed watching someone playing tennis as much as Federer. I'm just in awe. Pete Sampras was wonderful but he relied so much on his serve, whereas Roger has it all, he's just so graceful, elegant and fluid – a symphony in tennis whites."

Martina Navratilova (Former WTA Player): "I've been asked who I would pay to watch to play tennis, and Roger would be one of the few."

Fabrice Santoro (Former ATP Player): "I like Roger Federer to beat the record of 14 in Grand Slams. To beat this record, to win three more. So I'm always very happy when he goes through a Grand Slam. He's a very good guy on the court, he's fun to watch, and he's a great guy off the court."

David Goffin (ATP Player): "The greatest moment of my career was at the French Open, against Federer. It was the fourth round (2012). On the big court. It was great. (Did Federer say anything to you after?) Yes, there was a little speech on the court and it was very friendly. It was a great match and I had a hug with him. It was great...When I was young I had a lot of pictures of Roger Federer in my room."

Rene Stauffer (Author of "The Roger Federer Story: Quest For Perfection"): "When I first saw Roger Federer play tennis when he was a 15-year-old, I didn't think that I would even write his name in my newspaper, let alone a book about him."

Marcelo Rios (Former ATP Player): "When I was retiring from the ATP circuit (2003) he was only playing serve and volley. He didn't play that well from the baseline back then. Now he just won his fifth Wimbledon from the baseline and that shows that he is a really complete player. I think Federer is the best player and he is going to be the best player ever and hopefully he will."

Bjorn Borg (Former ATP Player): "Federer is a complete tennis player. He is an artist on the court and to beat him at Wimbledon in the best of five sets is almost an impossible task. I think and hope that Roger will equal my record this year – it could not happen to a better person. He has achieved so many great things in tennis and if he stays clear of injuries, stays motivated and continues at the same pace as he is doing, he will definitely be the greatest player of all time."

Ai Sugiyama (WTA Player): "I love to watch Roger. He's really like art. He really can do everything, serves great, returns good, so smart, groundstrokes, volleys, movement. It's just unbelievably smooth."

Jeremy Chardy (ATP Player): "My favorite player to watch is Roger. I love his game, I love his attitude."

Jo-Wilfried Tsonga (ATP Player): "When Federer enters the locker room, there is silence. You feel that the boss has just come in. He's cool, relaxed and loves teasing us nicely."

Mark Knowles (Former ATP Player): "Roger Federer, he's really amazing the way that he plays the game. It's kind of disheartening - he makes it look so easy but yet it's really special to watch him play. I've been lucky to be around some great tennis players - Sampras, Agassi and now Federer."

Tiger Woods (Pro Golfer): "Yeah, Roger came out and watched the back nine. We had dinner last night on the boat. He's obviously playing this week (at Key Biscayne). But it's great to have him out here. I think he's a wonderful supporter of golf, and I think it's pretty neat when you have probably the most dominant athlete on the planet out there in your gallery...Tennis is (more difficult to win at than golf) in the sense that if you're physically dominant, you can dominate somebody. In our sport, you can't physically dictate what somebody else is going to do. You can't all of a sudden hit a drive out there past him and say, Okay, I win the hole. That doesn't happen. So a person who actually is more physically gifted and physically dominant can actually just overpower somebody, and that just does not happen in our sport. So it's a little bit more difficult in that sense, golf-wise. But what he's done, you know, over the last three years, no one's ever done...He plays (golf), yeah. He played for a number of years and then got a rib injury for a while and he thought it was caused by golf, so he quit playing golf for a little bit and that's when his tennis took off. But he's playing a little bit more now, starting to get into it again and absolutely loves it. His mom is a hell of a player, she shoots in the 70's all the time, so it's in the family."

Stefan Edberg (Former ATP Player): "I think he can go another couple of years dominating the game with what he's got. There's really only one or two things that can stop him – obviously an injury, or something personal to happen. But if that doesn't happen, he's going to continue to dominate. In a way, it's quite nice to see because he plays such beautiful tennis. It's really beautiful to watch. I quite like the way Federer plays the game."

Pete Sampras (Former ATP Player): "It's nice to watch him, he's a smooth player, pleasant to watch, easy on the eyes. It seems like he wants it, kind of like I did. One of the misconceptions was that I wasn't competitive, I wasn't 'mean.' But I just showed it in a different way. And I think he has some of that in him too. Roger's got that mentality, that even keel. He doesn't get too high or too low. That helps when you want to be the best player in the world, no doubt."

Boris Becker (Former ATP Player): "I am convinced he will win many more Wimbledons, U.S. Opens and other Grand Slam titles. In a way, he has old-fashioned technique. He does not just play heavy topspin, he's very versatile. He can serve and volley, he can stay back, he can slice, he can play drop shots. He plays like they used to, like Ilie Nastase. He plays all the shots of tennis and that's something we don't really see anymore. He's amazing, he's just incredible. And if he stays healthy and motivated, he is the kind of guy that can overtake the greatest. I also like how Federer is very popular with other players and with the media. He is a very sociable guy."

Rod Laver (Hall of Famer): "Roger's got too many shots, too much talent in one body. It's hardly fair that one person can do all this — his backhands, his forehands, volleys, serving, his court position...the way he moves around the court, you feel like he's barely touching the ground, and that's the sign of a great champion. And his anticipation, I guess, is the one thing that we all admire."

Rene Stauffer: "This is a guy who buys drinks for photographers and thanks reporters who show up to his press conferences. Roger lives that saying: 'It's nice to be important, but it's important to be nice."

Martina Hingis (Former WTA Player): "We never played together during our younger days however, I do remember that he was my ball boy at one of the Basel tournaments (laughs). That was funny. The only time we played together was at the Hopman Cup a few years ago. We won when we played together. He was a great partner. I get to see him play fairly often. Whenever I switch on the TV, you see Roger playing. I love to see him play."

Sjeng Schalken (Former ATP Player): "I like him as a person and I like him as a sportsman."

Lisa: "I work in the players lounge cafeteria (at U.S. Open), and we all agree many of the players are kind of spoiled, they get everything done for them, they get limo rides to the hotels, they get pampered here, massages before and after matches, they get their clothes washed, and many of them aren't very nice to us, they don't talk with us. Federer is nice though. He is one of the only ones I can say is nice. Yeah, I like Federer."

Andy Roddick (ATP Player): "He's so talented, some of the things he does out there, you wonder, Is this humanly possible? I'm sure every time he walks out on court, he feels like he's going to win...I almost wish I could hate him but I can't, he's too nice."

Greg Norman (Pro Golfer): "I'm a huge Roger fan. Obviously because of his grace and perfection of the game. Watching him hit a backhand is like standing there looking at the Mona Lisa all the time – it's almost perfect. So, in sport, you always get these one-every-thousand-year athletes – we've seen it in golf with Jack Nicklaus, and we've seen it in tennis with probably Roger Federer right now. And if you have the opportunity to see him live and what he can do – it's totally different live than it is on TV, there's no question about it. And seeing him more than once live...he's just an incredible talent."

Serena Williams (WTA Player): "I wish I could play like Roger Federer. Roger is just, like, unbelievable...he's just so perfect out there."

Marat Safin (Former ATP Player): "He's a magician."

Gaston Gaudio (Former ATP Player): "He's a genius."

Mark Knowles (Former ATP Player): "The superlatives that you can use to describe Roger are endless."

Sania Mirza (WTA Player): "I like to watch Roger. He's amazing to watch. I think he's fun to watch and learn from, it looks like he's kind of playing music. He's like an artist and he kind of just glides on the court. And he does whatever he wants with the ball."

Tennis Blogger: "Pure, rich, dripping and abundant talent. I have never seen that much of it ever, since boxer Muhammad Ali and soccer player Pele. Although I have seen videos of the latter two, witnessing it first hand from Federer is like an out-of-body experience. If you have not seen him in action in person, you are not just depriving yourself of tennis genius, but also of absolute beauty in its purest form. If you admire anything beautiful, you don't need to know the mechanics of the form it is in, to appreciate it. Like, you don't have to be a boxing fan, to enjoy the arsenal of shots and more importantly how effortlessly and elegantly they are executed, in the ring by Muhammad Ali. If you love beauty and grace, you cannot miss it irrespective of the form and character it manifests itself in. If you have not already done it, go out and buy the ticket to Federer's next match. It doesn't matter if you are a tennis fan or not. You are not going out to watch a tennis match, you are watching genius at work – a once in a lifetime kind of euphoria. It is not everyday that a genius is born. History is proof that the medium through which that genius is expressed is irrelevant. It is a spectacle to behold even for a layman."

Danny Casesa (U.S. Open ballperson): "Federer was playing a match against Marcos Baghdatis and he turned around and said, 'I'm so fucking off!!' So I turn around to the line judge and I say, 'I wish I was that fucking off.' And I kinda guess I said it louder than I guess I should have. And then he ended up hearing me and turned around and said, 'Thank you.' Anyway, the guy in the middle of a match, he didn't need to turn around and say anything. Just the fact he acknowledged what I said and was still nice about it."

Stefan Koubek (ATP Player), when asked his tennis inspirations: "The first one was Boris Becker. Then I switched to Michael Chang and Agassi. And, right now, there's only one, he's a good friend of mine, but he's the best player in the world, which is Roger Federer. To watch him every time is something nice. Just to watch him play is amazing."

Marion Bartoli (WTA Player): "Roger is so nice all the time. He just...you're going into the player's lounge or you see him, he's waiting, he'll just say hello to you, ask you how you feel, every time. He's just so nice."

Dennis Kudla (ATP Player): "My inspiration is definitely Federer. Just looking at everything he's done, you love him. You want to be just like him. So you work toward that goal."

Danai Udomchoke (ATP Player): "I want him to make the record (of 15 total Grand Slams). I want him to win the French Open also. He's a good guy. He's a very good guy. He's very nice guy and he talk to everyone and he remember everyone. We are same age and then we play junior together. Once I play him, but in doubles, when we were like 16, 17. (Who won match?) He won [smiles]."

Dubai Ballboy: "I had a chat with Federer in Dubai. Federer was the most intimidating player to ballboy for, not in his behavior but more the fact I was so worried about doing something wrong. Speaking to him off the court, he was so cool. But he was just such a different person as soon as he was on court. So focused, zoned in, but still this incredible aura of calm."

Anthony Causi (New York Post photographer): "Shooting Federer is not like shooting anybody else. He's cold as ice. He doesn't show any emotion. When you shoot a guy like Blake, they're always blasting out or going wild during the match. Federer is cool and calm until the very end. He comes in as a surgeon, he does his job and he's out. I think he's one of the most intense guys to shoot. Because you really have to be good at what you do to shoot him, because he doesn't give you much emotion or anything. Just pure excitement in his game. He's a master of his game...Sampras was emotional. You saw it on his face if his game was off or if he wasn't performing the way he wanted to – you'd see that look on his face. Like most other guys who are playing the game today. Federer is just on his game all the time."

Chinese Journalist: "In China we call Federer 'The Eagle.'"

Igor Kunitsyn (ATP Player): "If I can't win I like to see Roger win. He wants it more than anybody else. He deserves it."

Dimitry Tursunov (ATP Player): "So many funny memories in tennis...let me think...I guess in Toronto, when I had Roger's bag before a match and he came back off the court after his interview, and he coudn't find his bag. That was pretty good [smiles]."

Tracy Singian (Wilson marketing mananger and former WTA player): "Everyone knew that Roger Federer was special. It's always a big question mark if someone will realize their true potential. Not only did Roger realize his potential, he exceeded everyone's expectations and continues to amaze year after year. Just when everyone has already written him off (in 2012), he reclaims the Wimbedon title and No. 1 ranking to set yet another record. There has never been anyone in the game to set a standard so high on and off the court. My respect for Roger grew exponentially after seeing him do his media prior to the start of Wimbledon. He's defending champ and he looks relaxed and happy to engage in the interviews. He gives his undivided attention... in five different languages! You can tell he truly enjoys the entire process and looks like there is no other place that he would rather be than in tennis. Don't really remember any former #1 players really putting in the time and effort he does. It's really set an example for the 'Next Generation' of players. But probably the thing I get a kick out of most is watching players watch Roger practice. You never really see other players just be in awe of other players... except when it's Roger. And on top of that, players - his peers want their own pictures with him. Maybe it's how social media has changed the way we communicate... but you know history is being made when most of these ATP & WTA players are coming up to Roger like a fan to make sure they document it. You know they will say, '...I was playing when...'"

Richard Berankis (ATP Player who practiced with Federer in Dubai for two weeks): "He gave me a lot of advices. But I think the main thing that I learned is to be a simple person. Cause he's like the God of tennis right now. And he's very simple, not arrogant at all, but he could be. And he's not. And I think that's the main thing that I learned from him."

Donald Young (ATP Player): "Federer came up to me actually, in the locker room, when I first turned pro, gave me a handshake and said 'Hello, keep up the good work.'"

Filip Peliwo (2012 ITF Junior No. 1): "I met Federer at the Champions' Dinner at Wimbledon, he spoke to me as if he knew me for years. He is such a great person, really takes time to talk to everybody. I definitely gained a lot of respect for him after that encounter. He is truly a class act."

Janko Tipsarevic (ATP Player): "I was practicing with him the other day. I was really enjoying him kicking my ass. First four games, I tell you – I won one point. Was unbelievable. Like on PlayStation."

Dominik Hrbaty (Former ATP Player, when asked for the funniest ATP players): "I think Roger is a very funny guy. We used to play a lot of doubles together, all the tournaments together. We did a lot of crazy stuff together. That kind of sense of humor that you do with your friends, it never can hurt you or whatever. You always take it as a good joke. (Just at that moment, Federer walks by in the locker room and says with a smile 'No interviews in here!') You see [laughs]?! So he can never really make an offense that can hurt your feelings."

Rafael Nadal (ATP Player) "Roger is the best, probably the best ever. It is Federer and the rest of us...He is a very nice person and a great competitor. I have a good relationship with him. I really admire what he does, how he plays, and how he behaves on and off the court. He is a role model for many people. I always had a bit of a language barrier with him because my English is not very good. But from time to time, and especially when there are important things to talk about, we sit and talk."

Xavier Malisse (ATP Player): "Federer is my toughest opponent. Before you are playing, you feel 4-love behind. He plays the game really quickly. So you have no breath."

Pete Sampras (Former ATP Player): "I think he has everything. It's just a question of how much he's willing to sacrifice to win majors. He's got all the tools, no question, he has a complete game. For the next four or five years, his competition will be the record books. I really believe in my heart that he's going to win way more than 14. I think the way he's going and the fact that he doesn't really have players really pushing him, he can win close to 17, 18 majors. He's going to slide by me and hit Nicklaus (18 total major wins) soon. The way he's dominating, it's unbelievable."

Andre Agassi (Former ATP Player): "He's the best I've ever played against. Pete was great but there was a place to get to with Pete. There's no such place like that with Roger. When a champion has two things they can count on out there as the best in the world – they're a dominant champion. Roger has closer to five. Every part of his game is something you've got to deal with – his speed, his shot-making ability, forehand, return, sense of the court, and his ability to raise his game. The guy brings so much, you just marvel at it. You get the feeling when you're looking at him, you're watching history."

Jim Courier: (Former ATP Player): "It's the biggest cheer I ever heard by an American crowd for a non-American player in an American stadium." (August 18, 2012 as Federer walked onto the court to face Novak Djokovic in the final of Cincinnati.)

John McEnroe (Former ATP Player): "The most beautiful player I've ever seen, with movement like Baryshnikov, like a dancer...He's such a true lover of the sport and he's such a class guy. And also I like seeing a little more emotion. We saw how devastated he was at Wimbledon. I felt like that was the proper thing to do at that time. So maybe, I think, you appreciate how great he was, because you see how difficult it can be for him sometimes. And how much it means to him. And that's good for us (the media), people that are in the sport. To see a guy who's accomplished so much, that loves it so much, that still wants it so badly...Roger's gonna have so much crowd support in the next couple of years. He got the biggest hand in The Parade of Champions (ceremony at 2008 U.S. Open). People know that, they see that the guy is actually human. People lost sight of it. It's pretty nice to see some guy fighting his heart out."

Novak Djokovic (ATP Player): "(At 2009 U.S. Open) I don't think you can ever get your game to the level of perfection. Only if you're Federer [smiles]."

Rod Laver: "(In July 2012) Roger Federer certainly is my claim to be the best of all time if there is such a thing. Roger's got all the shots, his anticipation is unbelievable, his timing off the ground strokes with his shots, his single-handed backhand is one of the best there is. But at the same time, I look at Rafael Nadal and what he's done to win seven French Open titles and Wimbledon. Being able to play with somewhat of a suspect knee, his way of motoring around the court and tracking shots down is quite uncanny. They're very close. Are they great champions and do they have equal abilities? I'd say yes, they're pretty much equal."

Chapter 2: First Memories of Federer by ATP Players

Nathan Healey played Roger Federer in a junior tournament when both were still teenagers...

Question: You beat Roger Federer when you were 16?

Nathan Healey: "That's correct. It was in Switzerland, under 16 tournament. I was 16, Roger was 15. I'm pretty sure it was 6-4 in the third. I'm undefeated against Roger Federer, so that's my claim to fame [smiles]."

Question: Does he remember this match?

Nathan Healey: "I think he does. These guys remember so many matches it's unbelievable. He was coached by an Australian you would know, Peter Carter. He did a fabulous job with him. He was with him at the time. It was a good tournament for me."

Question: Any standout memories from this match? Did you see him becoming the great player he is?

Nathan Healey: "Not at that stage. I think I vaguely remember his game was similar to mine. Single-handed backhand, didn't mind getting forward. We had a battle out there. Outdoor red clay."

Question: Do you remember what you did that worked against him?

Nathan Healey: "I can't remember details like that [smiles]. I could make something up but I can't really remember. I can picture the court that we played on. It was a good tournament for me. I went through one of the seeded players after that. I can't remember his name."

Question: What do you think Federer did to become such an exceptional, outstanding player?

Nathan Healey: "I think he had the tools. I think he just developed that over time. But the foundation was built by Peter Carter and he kept on developing it. And when Peter Carter died, there was something that clicked. I'd love to know what it was. There was something that clicked mentally, that brought it all together for him. And I'm fascinated by that side of the game - the mental side. I like to think of it as he's almost playing in a meditative state. He's just out there executing strategies, he's not thinking, he's very present. He's not thinking ahead or behind. He's not worrying about the score or what can come of the result. It's pure present for him. That's how I feel he plays. And I think he's one of the very few that actually understands that."

Question: Before your match with him do you remember your mindset going in and what you knew about him?

Nathan Healey: "Oh, I was crazy back then [smiles]. I feel he was a little bit of a hothead and didn't fully understand the mental side at that stage. I mean, he had great mentals around him that helped him over the time and guided him. There was something when he was on the Tour, he was sort of cruising around 50 or 60 in the world. There was something that happened and I think it had to do with Peter Carter's death in South Africa."

Question: A lasting memory or image of Roger Federer for you? Maybe a conversation?

Nathan Healey: "He remembers. Like the amount of people and players that he meets and plays against. It's fascinating that every time he sees me, he knows exactly who I am. Throughout the junior years we did see him a lot and sort of play with him. But when someone goes off and you don't see them for a few years, you feel like they'll slip from your memory. But he always remembers me, remembers my name."

Question: Talk a bit?

Nathan Healey: "Yeah, yeah, but around the tournaments, it's business. So he doesn't hang around the side. So it's more sort of passing conversation, just small talk. Always pleasant. He's a great ambassador for the sport, I think."

Bohdan Ulihrach: "I played Roger Federer. I never won a set [laughs]. We played three or four times. I remember one of our meetings was in Rotterdam. Eight years ago. He was already No. 1. And our first meeting was in Hamburg. It was cold, the April tournament in Hamburg. We played court one. He was not top 10, maybe not top 20. He was young but everybody knew he will have a big future. It was tough to play him. He was playing well, good, good serve, he can play any surface. I played him indoor and on clay. I never won a set."

Question: A lasting memory you have or Roger, on or off the court?

Bohdan Ulihrach: "I met him two years ago when I played club matches in Switzerland. I played for a team in Montreaux. And we played in Zurich and he was practicing there. It was like the week before Montreal. He was practicing there and I was coming into the locker room. I knew that he was there but I thought that maybe he will not remember me. And I was surprised he came to me and said, 'Hi Bohdan, how are you? Long time...' And we talk mostly about the kids. Because he has one-year-old twins, I have two kids. So we talked for like 15-20 minutes. So it was nice."

1999 Rotterdam R16 Federer 4-6 5-7

2002 Hamburg R32 Federer 3-6 0-6

2002 Vienna Q Federer 3-6 3-6

2005 Rotterdam R32 Federer 3-6 4-6

Patrick Rafter: "I kicked his ass [smiles]. French Open (1999), he was 17. And they said the kid's good. But he's a little bit soft in the head. I went over there. I lost the first set, 7-5 and I was really hacked off. And I broke him early in the second. And it all got a little too tough for him. So it was like 0-2-1 or something like that (actually, 5-7, 6-3, 6-0, 6-2). So he wasn't quite there just yet. But he obviously showed all the abilities. Then I played him a couple of years later (2001 in Miami) and he was still a little bit intimidated (Rafter won 6-3, 6-1)."

"He was a good mate for the Aussies, he was coached by an Australian guy (Peter Carter) and I was another Australian guy he sort of looked up to. We always got along well. Then the next time we played (2001 in Halle) you could see he was starting to lose it (intimidation factor) and he was just starting to get my measure and I thought, It's time to retire [smiles]." (Rafter won the Halle match 4-6, 7-6 (6), 7-6 (4).)

Question: What are the biggest ways you've seen his game change since the first time you played him?

Patrick Rafter: "He's older now. He's tougher mentally. His game was always getting developed. Any player starting off in a career, their games evolve and they get stronger and in the first couple of years you're sort of finding things out and finding out where you fit and working out your game. And working at how hard you have to train. And it can be very tough mentally. And it took time before his shots became really good shots. And that's what happened."

Question: Can you share any personal memories or interaction with Roger, something that maybe captures his essence?

Patrick Rafter: "We used to try to get him on the beer a bit. I remember in Germany - who the hell was there? - yeah, he was very nice. I used to try to get him out on the...come on mate. He used to love hangin' out with the Aussies but we were probably a little too hard for him, maybe we were trying to soften him up [smiles]."

Question: Do you see him continuing to win a major a year till he's 35 or do you think Andy Murray or Novak Djokovic will take over?

Patrick Rafter: "I don't see it. I called him to win one more Grand Slam after he hadn't won one for a couple of years. I thought he'll win another one. Like Pete (Sampras) sort of did. Everyone wrote Pete off. But when you're an amazing player - I like to use the word freak, but in a really good way - you do those type of things. But if you're a player like me where you're not that...you don't do that sort of thing. He might win one more - but I can't see him dominating anymore."

Pete Sampras: "First memory of Roger...not one specific moment. I just know, generally, he was a young kid growing up from Switzerland. Had some up and down results. I remember just seeing the name and obviously he's done okay [smiles]."

John McEnroe: "My first memory was just hearing about him. Just that he was the 'Next Guy.' And always wanting to see the guy because I'd heard but not seen. The first time I actually saw him - one of the first was probably, I think, one time I saw him in Europe, Davis Cup. We played (Switzerland), I guess I was lucky that I resigned from captaining. And then the first match that my brother (Patrick) ended up doing was playing some nobody named Federer in Switzerland. And watching and thinking this guy could actually do something. I didn't know if he'd be winning 17 Grand Slams but the guy certainly had it all."

Question: Remember the first time you spoke with Roger?

John McEnroe: "I can't, no. No. I barely remember yesterday [smiles]."

Andre Agassi: "I played him in Basel, Switzerland. I played two Swiss players back to back. Then I played Roger second round (Andre won 6-3, 6-2). I just never would have guessed he was in for the career he's had. He looked like he was trying to imitate Sampras when I first played him. But he just didn't look as good. He couldn't quite serve as big, he looked like he was not decisive enough about if he wanted to play coming in, if he wanted to play at the baseline. And so I was like, you never know if someone is going to evolve. So I didn't really give him much of a chance to be at the top. But he proved me wrong [laughs]."

Jim Courier: "My first memory of Roger Federer - I met him at an exhibition at River Oaks in Houston in 2000. And he was with Peter Lundgren at the time. And I remember meeting him at the sponsor player party and he was a pony-tailed kid I had heard a lot about but hadn't seen much of. And he had a really kind of laid-back manner about him. You didn't really see an eye of the tiger, you just heard that he was incredibly gifted."

Question: Did you ever hit with him or play tennis with him?

Jim Courier: "I never have. I hope to at some point. Roger is as easy as they come with that stuff, I've just never asked him. But in Australia, I've been on the court next to him plenty of times, when he's practicing on an off day. I'll slide in there at some point and hit a few with him."

Question: Do you remember a conversation or a time with him that captures his essence maybe?

Jim Courier: "I haven't spent any really significant time with Roger. Very cordial, couldn't be nicer when we see each other in passing, there's a sincerity in the conversation but I've never been to dinner with him. Never really spent a lot of time with him."

John Skelly: "I was coaching Vince Spadea in 1999. Spadea got into the ATP top 20 for the first time in 1999 and we went to Europe for the fall swing. Spadea draws some 18-year-old kid named Roger Federer in first round in Vienna, Austria. Federer schools Spadea in straight sets 6-4 6-2 and after the match old man Vince Spadea Sr. fires me on the spot and says to me quote unquote, 'This guy Federer sucks! He ain't never gonna be nothing.'"

Gilad Bloom: "One of the advantages of being the manager of a tennis academy ten minutes away from the U.S. Open is that when it was raining and matches get canceled at the Open, that's when players from the tournament are calling, wanting to use the indoor courts in the club. Paul Annacone, Roger Federer's coach, was on the line. 'Hey, Roger needs a court to train before the quarterfinals against Tsonga, you have room?' 'Come over, we'll find a court for him,' I told Annacone. The rumor spread around the club, the women put make-up on, the kids got their pens and papers ready, and the phenomenon arrived with an entourage which included Annacone, his trainer, a practice buddy and his father. 'Nice to meet you, Mr. Federer,' I introduced myself at the beginning of his practice, as Roger did his stretching exercises on the court. 'Welcome to the club.' 'Where did your curls go?' Roger surprised me with this question. 'Where do you remember me from?' I asked. 'What do you mean? I remember you when you played Basel, I was your ballboy, you had long and curly hair, where did your hair go, Gilad?' Federer asked me a question several taxi drivers in Tel Aviv had asked me over the years. So, now I have something to add to my resume, Roger Federer – and he formally acknowledges it as well, was my ball boy."

Johan Kriek: "I only met Roger a few years ago at Wimbledon as I was getting my bag checked at the players entrance to Wimbledon. I turned around and he was behind me waiting for the security people to finish my bags. I said, 'Hi Roger, I am Johan Kriek. I have never met you, nice to meet you.' He said, 'Of course, I know who you are, nice to meet you.' Later, I was told by a Wilson rep in South Africa that Roger told him that he used to find videos of my backhand so he could see why I could hit such angles, flip topspin lobs and slice the balls. Interesting."

Tim Smyczek: "I never played him. One of the coolest things, a good memory was after I qualified for the U.S. Open in 2012. I was hitting with James Blake on Arthur Ashe and Fed was coming to kick us off. When the time was up he told me, 'Good job qualifying.' So I thought that was pretty surreal."

Question: Wow. Pretty cool that he knew.

Tim Smyczek: "I don't know how or why but yeah, he told me 'Good job.'"

Jan-Michael Gambill: "We played four or five times. First memory of Fed was definitely not the guy that you see out there today, the amazing champion and already a legend. He wasn't as focused and tended to let things get to him. Could be a little bit of a crybaby on the court, he broke racquets. He really overcame something that was in him and he got rid of it and was able to get the steel focus. The first couple of times that I played him I was so irritated at his diversity though I already knew he was gonna be so good because he had kind of every shot. Not only could he take it to you with big pace but he could slow it down. He could hit it high, slice it, he had a one-handed backhand that looked like it was gonna be THE world class backhand to copy and to look out for. He didn't really have any weaknesses early. His only weakness was his focus. And just being that I knew he was going to be something."

Question: What was your most memorable match with Federer?

Jan-Michael Gambill: "My most memorable match was the time I beat him I suppose. I beat him in Doha in the quarterfinals, which was not an easy task, to beat him after any first round. The strategy seemed to work for me that day. That's the most memorable for me. But I played him a number of times. I played him at the Hopman Cup, I played him at the French Open, played at a couple of other places."

Question: Can you share a lasting memory or anecdote of Federer off court?

Jan-Michael Gambill: "Personally, I think he's just always been a good guy off the court. He has, kind of, my way of thinking on the court: You do what you can to win. You play the best you can and whatever it takes to do that. It doesn't mean you're an asshole. You're competitive. But when you walk off the court, you can be a normal guy. He's just been a normal guy. If he sees you he says hello. He's never thought that he's bigger than himself. He does his work on the court. I respect that a lot and always have. He's an awesome champion. Awesome ambassador for this sport. We need him. The lasting memory I think is something that he's gonna carve out of tennis history. I think it's the lasting memory for everybody. What he's done and continues to do is just amazing. I think that it's never gonna fade. So that's impressive."

Question: Is there anything you dislike about Roger?

Jan-Michael Gambill: "I wouldn't say I know Roger enough to not like something about him. I've practiced with him. I've played him. Just that he beat my ass a few times. I didn't like that [laughs]."

2000 Roland Garros R64 Federer 5-7 3-6 3-6

2000 Stuttgart Masters R64 Federer 6-7 0-1 (ret.)

2001 Davis Cup Federer 5-7 2-6 6-4 2-6

2003 Doha Q Gambill 6-4 7-5

Chapter 3: Describe The Feeling Of Walking On Court To Play Roger Federer In A Tennis Match

As a serious tennis buff reading this book, you have probably seen Roger Federer play several times on television or live at an ATP World Tour event. To see Federer perform on a tennis court is one thing, to actually compete against him in historic arenas before millions of viewers worldwide is a totally different experience. In this chapter, ATP players will discuss their memories of the feeling of what it's actually like to walk on the court to play tennis against Roger Federer...

"I was playing my best and he sort of showed me a new gear."

James Blake: "Throughout most of his career, I felt his sort of prime coincided with my prime. Because I felt great going on the court, I was usually playing at my best. And he was the one guy that I would come up against, that there was still doubt in my mind where I could play my best possibly and still lose. That time in my career I felt if I was playing my best, I was going to win. And I felt like the ball and everything was in my hands. And he was the only guy who I felt like I have played well against - and still lost. I was playing my best and he sort of showed me a new gear. That was tough to deal with. I was thrilled to get my one win over him at the Olympics. I know he was still No. 1 in the world and still trying to win and wanted to win the Olympics but that was a thrill for me. But all the other matches - he showed me a whole new level."

Question: Lasting memory of Roger Federer off the court for you?

James Blake: "The one I'll always remember - when I broke my neck in Rome on a practice court, went to the hospital. Ended up there. My coach was with me and we were trying to get out of there. We left a couple of days later. The tournament doctor came and visited to check in on me - and he brought one note from one player - and it was Roger Federer. The rest of the American guys, when I got home, were calling and checking in on me and everything but the one note that I got in the hospital room saying 'I hope you get better. I'm really sorry to hear...' - was Roger Federer."

Question: Did you save it?

James Blake: "I didn't save it. I was dealing with the fact that I had a broken neck [laughs]. I was worried about that. But I'll always remember the fact that he took the time when he was trying to win that tournament, to write me a note, to wish me well. I still remember that. As soon as I came back on the Tour, I went and made sure to make a bee-line for him and say thank you so much. It means a lot to me that you actually cared about your fellow players."

2003 US Open R32 Federer 3-6 6-7 3-6

2005 Cincinnati Masters R64 Federer 6-7, 5-7

2006 Indian Wells F   Federer 5-7 3-6 0-6

2006 Miami Q Federer 6-7 4-6

2006 US Open Q Federer 6-7 0-6 7-6 4-6

2006 Masters Cup China F Federer 0-6 3-6

2007 Cincinnati Masters F Federer 1-6 4-6

2008 Australian Open Q Federer 5-7 6-7 4-6

2008 Beijing Olympics Q   Blake 6-4 7-6

2008 Paris Masters Q walkover

2009 Madrid Masters R16 Federer 2-6 4-6

2011 Cincinnati Masters R16 Federer 4-6 1-6

"Everybody likes to play against him."

Richard Gasquet: "For sure he's a big star in tennis, the biggest star in sports, so for sure it's an honor and a big feeling. You have to be ready, like, it's always a very good match, very interesting, nice. The biggest star in tennis today. So everybody likes to play against him."

Question: Your most memorable match against him?

Richard Gasquet: "I lost, for sure, a lot of times against him. I won in Monte Carlo. I remember the crowd was cheering for me a lot so it was very nice. And I won eight years ago in Monte Carlo. So this is my best memory against him. As I say, I lost a lot of times to him. I'm not the only one [smiles]."

2005 Monte Carlo Masters Q Gasquet 6-7 6-2 7-6

2005 Hamburg Masters F   Federer 3-6 5-7 6-7

2006 Indian Wells Masters R16 Federer 3-6 4-6

2006 Halle R16 Federer   6-7 7-6 6-4

2006 Wimbledon R128 Federer 6-3 6-2 6-2

2006 Toronto Masters   F Federer 6-2 3-6 2-6

2007 Wimbledon SF   Federer 5-7 3-6 4-6

2010 Paris Masters R 32 Federer 4-6 4-6

2011 Dubai SF Federer 2-6 5-7

2011 Rome Masters R16 Gasquet 4-6 7-6 7-6

2011 Paris Masters R16 Federer 2-6 4-6

2012 Madrid Masters R16 Federer 3-6 2-6

"His fans and the press make him sound a lot more threatening than he is."

Dmitry Tursunov: "It depends. If everyone talks about Roger as being the greatest, then you come out on the court against him feeling a little threatened. So you start making a little bit of mistakes that you normally don't do. So I think a lot of it sort of happens in your head. You think to yourself a little bit, you force yourself to play too good for your own level. And if you get used to playing him, then you start playing a little bit within yourself and usually that's the best chance for you to do your best. It doesn't matter who you're playing, if you're trying to force yourself to play outside of your comfort zone, you're always going to make mistakes, whether it's against Roger, my grandmother, it doesn't matter, so."

"Obviously, he's a great player. There's no point in denying that. He's able to play consistently, play well consistently, he's a very good tactician, so if something doesn't work for him, he's able to switch the game patterns. He's able to come into net, he's able to slice, he can hit topspin. He can be aggressive, he can be defensive. So that allows him to be very flexible with his gameplans."

Question: What was your most memorable match with him?

Dmitry Tursunov: "I think, again, usually when you ask players like that it makes it sound like you played against such a great player. We're all professionals. The guy can do a lot of things better than me but it's not like playing him is such an awe-inspiring moment, like you meet Jesus for the first time in your life. And I think that's what a lot of people tend to make it to be. His fans and the press make him sound a lot more threatening than he is. And he's a very good player, there's no doubt about that. But again, he's lost plenty of matches. And it's not that you don't have a chance going out against him. He's a very good tactician. Physically he's talented. But he's not the most talented person in the world. He has great timing. He's able to slice and he's able to use his slice in an offensive way which not a lot of people can do."

"But again, the most memorable moment...I've played three matches against him. I've lost all three of them. In one of them, I did take a set off of him. In my last match against him, it was in the Olympics. I kind of defeated myself there in that final set. I was so nervous playing him that I made a lot of mistakes and all he had to do was show up on the court. If that makes him the greatest player of all time - by forcing players to shit their pants when they come out to play against him, then I guess that's the definition of a great player. And I'm not a great player. But I think I probably have the same effect maybe at a lower level. If I come out playing in Challengers, maybe I'd put a lot of pressure on the person. He's thinking, 'Oh f***, it's Tursunov, he's won two rounds at an ATP tournament last week. Now I have to do something extra to beat him.' And that's not the case. And a lot of times I beat players like that."

"Again, I'm not trying to downsize Roger and he doesn't need downsizing. I don't think it's necessary to bring him up to like a deity level of a player. He's not. He's defeatable. And Rafa's proved it. Rafa doesn't get affected by that. Mentally, he's very disciplined. He's able to just play his game pattern regardless of who he's playing. He could be playing you, me, Roger, he doesn't care. If Jesus comes down and starts floating on the court, he still plays the way he's playing. And that's why he's able to defeat Roger, in large part. There's a lot of other things. It's not like Rafa doesn't have any weapons. My point is, a lot of defeats against Roger happen psychologically. Players force themselves to step out of their comfort zone and they start making mistakes. It's like going out on a date with a really hot girl. You're probably going to try to make stupid jokes and then you're going to feel like an idiot after that. That's kind of how it feels. Just to sum it up [smiles]."

Question: Your lasting memory of Roger on court or off court? An anecdote?

Dmitry Tursunov: "Well, he can't. He's got an image to uphold. So he can't do anything less than, you know, like his hair is glowing."

Question: But you stole his bag once and hid it on him?

Dmitry Tursunov: "I did, in Toronto. I think that's probably why I got the set off of him [smiles]. I mean, he's a pretty mellow guy off the court. I'm pretty sure that he knows that he's really good in tennis and he's got a lot of records. And I think of Roger showed up at the Corona Bar (adjacent to our interview at a practice court at SONY Open in Miami) we'd have like 15 heart attacks in the Corona Bar. And people would just start praying and, but, I think, again, it's a part of the image. And a lot of it is press and how you present yourself. I really can't say any anecdotes because he's not going to put himself in a position where he can be embarrassed in some way. He's not gonna fart in front of people [smiles]. And then, after a certain amount of time, you start feeling like Roger never farts. So that's probably the anecdote in itself. That he's never farted in his lifetime. He never has to take a shower after his match. He doesn't smell. He smells like vanilla [laughter]."

2006 Miami Masters   R16 Federer 3-6 3-6

2006 Toronto Masters R16 Federer 3-6 7-5 6-0

2008 Beijing Olympics R64 Federer 4-6 2-6

"To be honest, I prefer to play Federer than to play Nadal or Djokovic. Because they make you suffer on the court."

Gilles Muller: "Well, it's always a nice feeling Roger because it's what you work for, those moments to play on the stadium, big court, against a guy like Roger. It's always an amazing feeling. It's actually nice to play him because you go on court and you know you have nothing to lose, you have everything to win. And if you lose 0 and 0 it's not a bad thing actually. It's not the end of the world. If you beat him or you get a close match with him, it's fun. I enjoy those moments. I've always been one of those guys who loved to have those big matches and I always played well in them. So I'm always looking forward to have those matches."

Question: Is Roger very hard for you to play against?

Gilles Muller: "Of course. He's one of the greatest of all time, if not the greatest. And obviously he's a very good player. To be honest, I prefer to play him than to play Nadal, for example, or Djokovic. Because they make you suffer on the court. They make you physically suffer on the court. And Roger's more the guy who hits winners. So it's not as hard physically to play him. That's what I felt. Of course, in tennis, of what he's able to do with the ball - it's just amazing."

Question: What is your most memorable match with Roger?

Gilles Muller: "The one I remember the most is the one at the U.S. Open when I lost in three close sets in quarterfinals. The first time I played him was pretty amazing too. I played him the first time in Indian Wells. That was back in 2005. And he had his long hair [laughs]. That was a pretty nice moment also because it was only my first year at the high level playing the big tournaments. So that was a nice moment. I like to remember the time we played at the U.S. Open because that was a close match, at least close to winning one set. So far, I've never won a set against him. So I was very close there."

Question: How are your relations with Roger off court?

Gilles Muller: "Well, he's very laid back. I mean, he's always friendly to everybody, so that makes him special. Because you have a lot of those guys you barely see and they barely talk to you. And that's probably also because we speak the same language. He speaks French-German like me too, so it's easy to communicate with him. He's a pretty nice person. He's laid back. You don't feel like he's mad at stuff all the time. He seems like...I've never seen him in a bad mood. That makes him a pretty good person I think."

Question: Can you share a lasting memory on or off court, maybe a conversation or an anecdote?

Gilles Muller: "I spoke to him the day before we played in the quarterfinals at the U.S. Open. And I was just surprised. Because, for me, it was the first time I was at that stage in the tournament. All the press work with all the interviews and everything. And because I'm coming from a country where they're not traveling to the tournaments so I have to make calls all the time and speak and give interviews in three or four different languages. So that's always tough for me. At that point, that was the first time that happened to me, so it was very tough for me. On the other hand, I just saw him and he was doing the same thing. And I guess he was doing that everyday. I was just asking how he does it. It was pretty nice to speak with him. I mean, he could have not answered to me, because we played each other the next day. I think there's a couple of guys who would not like to do that - speak to the guy or be nice to the guy you play the next day. But he was just very relaxed and he told me, 'Yeah, you get used to that. And it's tough, but...' But it was nice. It was a nice memory."

Question: Your first memory of Roger Federer?

Gilles Muller: "I think...I can't remember against who he was playing but I'm pretty sure it was at the Basel tournament and I watched it on TV. And everybody was talking about this Federer guy being the next No. 1 and being a very good junior. And I just remember that the racquet flew everywhere on the court [laughs]. He threw his racquet like almost every point he lost. And then people said that's one of his problems, he used to be crazy on the court, and very emotional. It's amazing how he developed in that manner. He's so calm on the court now, you barely see him say a word on the court now. That was pretty funny. I remember watching that match. I can't remember who he played but the guy hit a winner against him and he just threw the racquet from the baseline to his bag. I thought that was pretty funny because when you see him now he's a totally different person."

2005 Indian Wells Masters R32 Federer 3-6 2-6

2005 Bangkok   Q Federer 4-6 3-6

2008 U.S. Open Q   Federer 6-7 4-6 6-7

"On the last changeover I came over and sat with him. And I told him, 'Roger, finally you beat me. This is the day."

Dominik Hrbaty: "Roger is different. He's the new generation. He was comparable to Marcelo Rios, very talented, he has great hands, but the difference was Roger had the big serve, big return. He could make winners out of anything basically. And even out of defense. And Roger is just one of a kind. It's always a special feeling to play Roger or any No. 1 in the world. Because he's the best player in the world and you want to be at your best. If you can beat him you become a part of the history of tennis. Because you don't often meet a No. 1 in the world. And if you beat him, everybody says Wow, congratulations. You make the news. All the friends suddenly text you. It's just such a good feeling. Also you can do it for yourself because you can prove that your own tennis can play against the top player in the world. And this is the point of tennis. If you can prove, not only to yourself, but also to the other people that you are learned on the level, you're really playing at the top. And people are looking to you, that you are the one that can play tennis."

Question: What was your most memorable match against Federer?

Dominik Hrbaty: "Probably in Cincinnati when I beat him as the No. 1 in the world. But there was also one in Wimbledon that was our last meeting. Because it was after my surgery, I didn't play well and this was the only time that he beat me. Because I beat him two times before. We were very good friends with Roger and he was always joking about when he was going to beat me. And in Wimbledon, that match, we sit on the bench together, which is very unusual. On the last changeover I came over and sat with him. And I told him, 'Roger, finally you beat me. So this is the day.' And we had a good laugh. It's not only about competition, sports and tennis is about friendship and also about, you know, making the thing that you will remember for the rest of your life."

2000 Paris Masters R64 Hrbaty 4-6 6-2 6-2

2004 Cincinnati Masters R64 Hrbaty 1-6 7-6 6-4

2008 Wimbledon R128 Federer 3-6 2-6 2-6

"It's always great to be with him on the court."

Tomas Berdych

"I said that many times, for me it's kind of a final of the tournament, you know, or celebration of tennis, I would say, because it's always great to be with him on the court, you know, with the results that he achieved and what a star he is. It's every single time for me, you know, 'the' match, you know, to be ready and to be really focused on. So, yeah, I like those matches so much. I would like to play with those guys every time."

Question: What's your most memorable match with Roger?

Tomas Berdych: "Well, definitely is the one from Wimbledon 2010 where it was the first time I beat him in the Grand Slam. You know, it was Wimbledon, so it was even more special to me. Yeah, it was first time that I won actually on the Centre Court in Wimbledon, as well. So, you know, it's been really a lot of, I would say the first moments of the match, and then, yeah, beating him there was something really incredible."

Question: Do you remember your first memory of Federer, maybe a conversation, on or off court? What's your first memory of Federer?

Tomas Berdych: "Well, it's from actually the Athens Olympics when I beat him first time. We came to the court for the warmup before the game, and actually we had a (problem because) they signed us on the same court at the same time. So we want to start, and he came and he said, 'Guys, I have this court.' I said, 'Yeah, but we have it, too.' Then he was like, 'Okay, so we will share.' And then he said, 'You know what? Let's split it. I will take the first half an hour and then you do the second one.' He said, 'Fine?' I said, 'Yeah, yeah, sure, of course. Go.'"

"It was actually the first time that I ever saw him that close. I was sitting next to the court watching him warm up and I was saying to my coach, 'What am I going to do with him? What should I do?' I was seeing him first time how he sees the ball, how fast he plays. My match with him was in couple of hours. I was like, 'Okay, what I'm going to do?' Actually I went on court to play him and I beat him. It was incredible for me."

2004 Athens Olympics R32 Berdych 4-6 7-5 7-5

2005 Hamburg R32   Federer 2-6 1-6

2006 Roland Garros R16 Federer 3-6 2-6 3-6

2006 Halle   F Federer 0-6 7-6 2-6

2006 Wimbledon R16 Federer 3-6 3-6 4-6

2007 Davis Cup Federer 6-7 6-7 3-6

2008 Australian Open R16 Federer 4-6 6-7 3-6

2008 Beijing Olympics R16 Federer 3-6 6-7

2009 Australian Open R16 Federer 6-4 7-6 4-6 4-6 2-6

2010 Miami Masters R16 Berdych 6-4 6-7 7-6

2010 Wimbledon Q Berdych 6-4 3-6 6-1 6-4

2010 Toronto Masters Q Federer 3-6 7-5 6-7

2011 Cincinnati Masters Q Berdych 6-2 7-6

2011 Paris Masters SF Federer 4-6 3-6

2012 Madrid Masters F Federer 6-3 5-7 5-7

2012 U.S. Open Q Berdych 7-6 6-4 3-6 6-3

2013 Dubai SF   Berdych 3-6 7-6 6-4

"I just enjoyed to play with this incredible person."

Denis Istomin: "Of course the first thing is you have to come on court and just try to fight against this guy because he's an incredible player, the best of the best. The first feeling is, of course, to play and fight and try to win. But it never happened, so it's difficult to win against him. We played like three times already. The first time was my first match in a Grand Slam, we played in the first round of the 2006 Australian Open. I just enjoyed our game and I just enjoyed to play with this incredible person."

Question: How do you feel you performed against him in the matches?

Denis Istomin: "The last match was really close first set. So I have some chances, break points on his serve. So he's just coming back and playing incredible shots. He never gives up. You have to be so concentrated and play more than you're best tennis to beat him."

Question: Do you feel you're getting closer and you are going to figure out how to do it?

Denis Istomin: "I hope so. Maybe one day I can come and play my best of best tennis and be close to win a set, first, then maybe match."

Question: Ever talk with Roger? Do you have an off-court memory of him?

Denis Istomin: "We're always talking, so we're always saying hi to each other and talk about something. He's a nice guy. It's nice to talk with him and he gives many chances to talk. He's a nice person. He has so much respect from me and from other players."

2006 Australian Open R128   Federer 2-6 3-6 2-6

2010 Cincinnati Masters R32   Federer 2-5, ret.

2012 London Olympics Federer 5-7 3-6

2013 Indian Wells R64 Federer 2-6 3-6

"He always changes up the game so you're really uncomfortable on the court."

Alexandr Dolgopolov: "I played him once in singles (2010 Basel R32). It wasn't the best match for me. But it's different. It's nice because he's such a great player. So it's really nice to compete with him and just try to play him, try to beat him."

Question: What is your first memory of Roger, ever practice? Chat?

Alexandr Dolgopolov: "We say hi but I don't think we practiced ever together. But we don't talk much, we just say hi, maybe a few words. He's cool. He's always polite, he's always nice to everyone. He's a pure Swiss guy [smiles]."

Question: What is it that's so hard to play against him?

Alexandr Dolgopolov: "I think it's tough because it's really tough to read the game. He just hits a normal backhand and it looks like it's pretty easy and slow - and the ball bounces different from other players. You get more pressure on your shots so you're not that comfortable to hit the ball after his shots. And he always changes up the game so you're really uncomfortable on the court. You need to be prepared with all kinds of shots. And he can always go forward and hit good volleys. It's always tough to be really fully focused."

Question: Did you have any success against him, a tactic that you were able to do that was working?

Alexandr Dolgopolov: "Doubles only [laughs]! We beat him in doubles."

Question: That was the Indian Wells final, right?

Alexandr Dolgopolov: "Yeah. Against him and (Stan) Wawrinka. Singles, as I said, I played him one time in Basel and it was pretty easy for him - 6-4 5-2 and I twisted my ankle. So I can't say I played a lot of time against him."

Question: What happened in that amazing Indian Wells final?

Alexandr Dolgopolov: "I think it was the best tennis we showed. With Xavier Malisse in doubles, we were just hitting every ball and everything was going in. And we won five matches in super tiebreaks. So we really didn't care if it was Federer and someone else. We were just hitting the balls as hard as we can - and making it. It was a fun match."

"He always tells me very good things about my game after the match."

Alejandro Falla: "Well, it's amazing to play Roger Federer. It's amazing how nervous you get because once you're walking on the court, everybody starts clapping and screaming when Roger's going on the court. So it's a very nice moment when I first play him. I think he's an idol for everybody and the people give support for him when he walks on court."

Question: He's an idol for you too, right?

Alejandro Falla: "Yeah. I think everybody recognizes what he does and he's current. And as a person, I think more than the results, as a person, it's amazing how he is, the way he is and how he acts with the people and the players."

Question: Can you share a memory of how he treated you off the court?

Alejandro Falla: "Off the court he's very nice to me. After every match we shake hands and he always tells me very good things about my game after the match. I see the kind of person for me and all the players and the people, when I see him on and off the court."

Question: You played one of your finest matches against him at Wimbledon in 2010. The famous five-setter. Your memories of it?

Alejandro Falla: "Yeah. It was an amazing match. I enjoyed that match so much. It was a shame I couldn't finish that up. But I learned a lot from that match and it's going to be in my memory forever."

Question: What did you learn from that match?

Alejandro Falla: "Personally, I think it showed me I could beat any player, because I was playing the best player ever on grass. He was No. 1 and it gave me a lot of confidence in my game. That's the main thing."

Question: What is special about Roger's game? What surprises you about his game?

Alejandro Falla: "He can do any shot. He's got every shot. His slice is amazing. He serves very well. Every shot, every stroke he's got is a weapon. He just can come up with anything you never expect."

Question: Is it extra difficult to play against someone you respect so much?

Alejandro Falla: "Yes. He's got a lot of respect from every player. I've heard something that Roger and Rafa and Novak, they win I think half of the matches before they walk on court. Because the respect for them is so high. I didn't respect him - maybe the first time - but then I learned from it, that first loss. And then I walk on court thinking I could beat him."

Question: Is Roger the hardest guy for you to play out of all the top players?

Alejandro Falla: "Well, I haven't played Rafa. My game, I think, bothers him a little bit. Because, well, the results show that. I haven't played Rafa but I think - I heard Rafa is a little tougher to play because he never gives up any ball. Roger, sometimes, he needs it - he has so much talent, he makes the break when he needs it and that's it. One break and you're done. But with Rafa - that's what I heard - he never gives up any points. So he's tough to play against. If you're playing bad against Roger maybe you can still have a chance to win a few games."

2004 Wimbledon R64 Federer 1-6 2-6 0-6

2006 Roland Garros R64 Federer 1-6 4-6 3-6

2010 Roland Garros R64 Federer 6-7 2-6 4-6

2010 Halle R16 Federer 1-6 2-6

2010 Wimbledon R128 Federer 7-5 6-4 4-6 6-7 0-6

2012 London Olympics R64 Federer 3-6 7-5 3-6

"He came off the court and he said, 'Bogie, congrats, it was an amazing year.'"

Alex Bogomolov Jr.: "I remember the first time I played him was Australian Open, the first year he won it. And I qualified fairly easy there. I think I lost a total of nine games in three matches, so I was going in very, very confident. In good shape. I remember we walked on the stadium court, the first couple of games were tight. And then after that, the third set was six-all and he wasn't even breaking a sweat and I was like fully drenched and everything. I just remember his slice was so aggressive, such an offensive shot that I couldn't do anything with the ball. And anytime he sliced the ball, the point was pretty much over because the next ball was an easy ball for him. That's the one memory I remember."

Question: The second match was in 2012. Your memories from that one?

Alex Bogomolov Jr.: "I played him last year in Cincinnati and from that match I don't think I had a break point. The last game, the way he was serving, I don't think he hit the same serve twice the whole match. Every serve had a different spin, a different objective that he wanted to serve with, for meaning. I just remember I had no chance on the returns."

Question: It sounds like he was even more difficult to play the second time than the first?

Alex Bogomolov Jr.: "Yeah, he's definitely gotten better, that's why he's the best player in the game, because he's developed all the shots in the game. He doesn't have one hole that you can particularly go to and think that you're going to win the point. He has every angle covered."

Question: Any lasting memory of him, on the court or off, any conversation?

Alex Bogomolov Jr.: "I remember in 2011 I got the ATP Most Improved Player Award. I went to London. And actually they presented me an award right after his first Round Robin match. And he came off the court and he said, 'Bogie, congrats, it was an amazing year.' So that was pretty cool. That was probably even better than the award itself."

2004 Australian Open R128 Federer 36 46 06

2012 Cincinnati R32 Federer 36 26

"I beat him in a practice set in Houston. One set. Then the next day his coach is asking me again to practice with him."

Yen-Hsun Lu: "You have to be ready to play one of the best tennis players in the world and he's one of the greatest tennis players now, and for me, I'm trying to be mentally fresh and don't kill myself, get nervous. Everybody will be cheering for him. But business comes with challenges and it's really kind of special and I'm trying to enjoy it more to play him. You have to try to bring your best tennis to him because he won't give you any chance with it, or free points. You have to prepare it by yourself and to make the opportunity to make a point. Against him and against the top four guys, you have to be ready, they will always give you pressure, even they try to crush you [smiles]. So all the mentally and physically you have to prepare for this match."

Question: How do you feel about your performances vs. Roger Federer?

2009 Wimbledon R128 5-7 3-6 2-6

2012 Shanghai Masters R32 3-6 5-7

Yen-Hsun Lu: "Beginning for sure, I feel nervous and tight. And after two games I feel relaxed again and I release the pressure. I know how I play I can compete with him. Fortunately after two games I have already the big goals and also I can use my speed and the court speed, so I get used to the tempo and all the things. Then I feel to myself: 'Oh, this is the chance to compete with him.' So then I try to play my best tennis and actually, in the end, I feel it was a good match. I lose both sets, one service game. I had a couple of chances, a few break points. But, I mean, he's still the No. 2 player in the world, lifetime he's the No. 1 player. So every time you get the chance, you have to try - or even sometimes you have to overplay - to make a point happen. If you can make the point happen maybe he feel the pressure. Then he can give you the free chance or other chances."

Question: What is your first memory of Roger?

Yen-Hsun Lu: "I met him November 2003 in Houston. And this time he was first time in the final eight in Houston (ATP World Tour Finals). I was there with Rainer Schuettler. And luckily I have the chance to hit with him. For me, first time meeting him, he was a nice guy, say hi to me. At this time my ranking was like 200 or something. But then I have good practice with him. Even in practice I beat him [smiles] in a practice set. One set. Then the next day his coach is asking me again to practice with him. I mean, he's not taking less serious in the practice but he's respecting all the players, it doesn't matter where you are ranking in this moment, 200 or 300 or even if you are top players, he's taking the same thinking for every player. I don't know him very well, deep or something but at least in the face, we practice a few times, he's always talking nice, even after practice he's waiting for you to leave the court together. He's that kind of guy. But I know, for sure, nobody will be perfect, for sure there may be some people that don't like him. But, for me, I have nothing to complain about him. And, for me, when I face him, he is acting really nice and he's a really respectable guy."

"Something changed in his mind - to become a champion."

Sebastien Grosjean: "My first memory of Roger was Marseille. He finished No. 1 junior at end of 1998 and he had a wildcard into Marseille. He took my wildcard! Because he couldn't play qualies because he was playing a Challenger the weekend before. Young player, everybody was talking about him in the juniors, talent and the technique and everything. And he beat Carlos Moya. He beat Moya in Marseille. It was amazing. That was a big win coming the first year on the Tour. Even if it was indoor, it was still against Carlos Moya. It was an impressive win."

Question: What was your most memorable match with Federer?

Sebastien Grosjean: "I would say it's maybe Wimbledon. The second year he won over there (2004). The year before he lost first round at the French (to Luis Horna) then he won Wimbledon. Then he start. He put everything together. His game was there. It was more his mental was something on or off. But at Wimbledon he was a different player than the year before. You could see the confidence in him going on the court, he was really focused on his game. He had everything. He could do every shot with his racquet. Was impressive."

Question: How many times did you play him?

Sebastien Grosjean: "I didn't play him a lot. Of course, I was beating him before he start to win Slams. He was really difficult to play. We played six or seven times. I won twice, maybe three or four times, something like that. It was hard to play against him. Even if you are playing his backhand, he can change the rhythm with his backhand. So he's someone who's tough to play against."

Question: When you first saw him play did you imagine he would become the great player he became?

Sebastien Grosjean: "At the beginning, yes, when he was 18 years. And then he had trouble, maybe after the pressure of all the expectations of everybody. With the comparisons of Pete Sampras and everything. But when he start to accrue everything you need to be a champion, like around 22 or 23, he start to be an amazing player."

Question: A lasting memory you have of Roger, on or off the court?

Sebastien Grosjean: "When he came on the Tour he was traveling with his

PlayStation, you know, playing video games at night. Sometimes he couldn't wake up in the morning because he played all night [smiles]. But because he was a kid he was enjoying the life. And then he became - something changed in his mind - to become a champion. He's really great for the game and the sport. He's a great ambassador. Nothing but respect."

Question: Was he the hardest player for you to play?

Sebastien Grosjean: "It's tough to say. Because I played Sampras on grass and he was tough also. I played Agassi. At that time they were the best players. Also, I played Nadal on clay [smiles]. So it's also tough. But those guys, the champions, it's tough to play against."

2001 Syndey Q Grosjean 7-5 6-4

2001 Rotterdam R16 Federer 6-4 3-6 4-6

2001 Monte Carlo Masters Q Grosjean 6-4 6-3

2004 Wimbledon SF Federer 2-6 3-6 6-7

2006 Toronto Masters R32 Federer 3-6 3-6

"It's a strange and special feeling to play Roger. I always look forward to play against him."

Gilles Simon: "What is the feeling on the court when I have to play Roger Federer? It's a strange feeling. Most of the time, for a player of my ranking, it's very special because it means that you won three or four matches, so it means that you are playing good. And you know that he is going to be very tough because he won also a lot of matches. And you know you're going to have the best Roger in front of you. It's always impressing, a little bit, even if now I'm starting to be used to it. But it's always on the center court, the crowd cheering only for him. So it's always tough conditions for us. But I think he deserves it. I always look forward to play against him."

Question: Your most memorable match against Federer?

Gilles Simon: "We always have a nice match...I would say the match in the Australian Open (2011). It was after I was injured (knee injury), I had a very low ranking and had to play him in the second round. Unfortunately I lost in five sets. But it was a very, very good match. And one of the best ones I ever played, I think."

2008 Toronto Masters R32 Simon 2-6 7-5 6-4

2008 Masters Cup China RR Simon 4-6 6-4 6-3

2011 Australian Open R64 Federer 6-2 6-3 4-6 4-6 3-6

2011 Miami Masters QF Federer 0-3 (ret.)

2013 Rome Masters R16 Federer 1-6 2-6

2013 French Open R16 Federer 1-6 6-4 6-2 2-6 3-6

"It's great fun to be on the court with the greatest player ever."

Lukas Dlouhy: "It's always great to be on court with Roger, even if you go for practice courts. It's so many people watching and you want to do the best performance on the court with him. Even if you're warming up or you're practicing between the matches or tournament. So I always enjoy it. It's great fun to be on the court with the greatest player ever."

Question: Your most memorable match with Federer?

Lukas Dlouhy: "Actually, I played him in Toronto and won with me partnered with Leander Paes. And we won. And they won the next week or week after at the Olympic Games. So it was a good experience for me."

Question: A lasting memory of Roger, on or off court?

Lukas Dlouhy: "He's a great guy. So you can just talk about him for many hours. I can say that we are friends and every time we meet each other it's fun and he says How's life and how's everything? So, really, a cool guy."

"I don't play against Federer, I play against the most perfect player."

Benoit Paire: "It was the worst. Because, for me, Federer is the most, the best player in the world. For me, when I'm against him on the court, it's tough, I don't play against Federer, I play against the most perfect player and it's very difficult."

Question: How do you feel you performed in your match against Federer?

Benoit Paire: "I feel so bad [smiles]."

2012 Basel Q Federer 2-6 2-6

2013 Australian Open R128 Federer 2-6 4-6 1-6

"We're pretty good friends off the court, so it makes it even more special."

Tommy Haas: "It's pretty awesome, especially playing somebody like him. We're also pretty good friends off the court, so it makes it even more special in some ways because we know we're going to have a lot of these matches to talk about down the road when we're both not playing anymore. And you feel how many balls can come at different angles and different speeds that you're likely to see many other players play."

Question: You're most memorable match with Roger?

Tommy Haas: "Now, I have to say the one in Halle that I won (2012) in Germany on Father's Day. My father was there. My father-in-law was there. Me being a dad. Against Roger in the finals. That's one of my most memorable ones. But we've had a couple of other good ones. The French Open when he came back after being down two sets to love, where I had maybe a good chance to take him. He came back and played really well. We've played some good ones in Australia. Couple of times actually. Back in 2000, in the Sydney Olympics. Then in 2002 Australian Open. 2006 I think, Australian Open was another one that was over five sets. So we've had some pretty amazing, good battles. So we always seem to have a pretty good match...he actually toyed with me a few times too. And here one year too, in Miami [smiles]."

2000 Sydney Olympics SF Haas 6-3 6-2
2000 Basel   R32   Federer 3-6 3-6
2002 Australian Open R16 Haas 7-6 4-6 3-6 6-4 8-6
2002 Paris Masters R16 Federer 2-6 6-7
2005 Halle   SF   Federer 4-6 6-7
2006 Doha SF   Federer 3-6 3-6
2006 Miami Masters R32 Federer 1-6 3-6
2007 Dubai   SF Federer 4-6 5-7
2007 Wimbledon R16 default loss
2008 Indian Wells Q default loss
2009 Roland Garros R16 Federer 7-6 7-5 4-6 0-6 2-6
2009 Wimbledon SF Federer 6-7 5-7 3-6
2012 Halle F Haas 7-6 6-4
2013 Halle SF Federer 6-3 3-6 4-6

"I was in awe."

Sam Querrey: "When I played him when I was younger, I was still kind of in awe and it was just kind of fun to be out there. I didn't think I was going to win."

Question: Your most memorable match with Roger?

Sam Querrey: "I have only played him twice. It was probably my match here in Miami. I lost to him in a night match here. That was the first time I played him. It was just so fun, such an experience, something I'll always remember."

Question: Were you pleased with that performance?

Sam Querrey: "Yeah, I think I lost like 6-3 6-4. I was pretty nervous. I don't think I expected to win back then. I was only like 18. I guess I was happy with it."

2007 Miami Masters R64 Federer 4-6 3-6
2008 Roland Garros R128 Federer 4-6 4-6 3-6

"17 Grand Slams - but you try to forget that."

Milos Raonic: "You walk out on the court to play the guy and you have a lot of respect for him. You'll hear it when they introduce the guy. It's not like they forget to say 17 Grand Slams, and so forth [smiles]. But you try to forget that. And you see the match as a guy trying to take away from you what you want. And you try to, in a respectful way, don't respect them on court too much."

Question: Your most memorable match with Federer?

Milos Raonic: "I think the one I played the best in was in Madrid (2012). It's tough to play him because he plays very well. He can do a lot of things [smiles]."

2012 Indian Wells Masters R32 Federer 7-6 2-6 4-6
2012 Madrid Masters R32 Federer 6-4 5-7 6-7
2012 Halle Q Federer 7-6 4-6 6-7
2013 Australian Open R16 Federer 4-6 6-7 2-6

"He changed a lot his mental approach to tennis."

Rainer Schuettler: "With Roger, what can you say, he's an unbelievable player. I know him for so long. And you always know if you play 100% and he's not 100% in shape, then maybe you have a slight chance to beat him. So against him you always have to risk everything. Go on court and hope he misses some. He's just an unbelievable player, great person, and it's always great to play him."

Question: What was your most memorable match with Roger?

Rainer Schuettler: "Well, I beat him in Dubai, I think 6-2, 6-1 one year, in 2001 or 2002. So though it was nice, I have to admit, afterwards, he played much better."

Question: How were you able to beat him that time?

Rainer Schuettler: "I think it was not his best day, I really played well, it was my best times and he was maybe not 100% fit, tight from playing a lot of matches. So I took the chance and I beat him."

Question: What is your first memory of Roger?

Rainer Schuettler: "I know when he was a junior I saw him playing and he was really breaking racquets and everything [smiles]. So he changed a lot. He really mentally changed a lot his approach to tennis. That's great to see. I know a little bit both sides of him."

Question: Why do you think he was so difficult at his best to play against?

Rainer Schuettler: "He has no weaknesses. He's moving unbelievable. He can play defensive from the baseline, he can go to the net, he can serve and volley. You never know with him what happens. And his game - it doesn't matter how you play, he always finds an answer for it. A lot of players out there, if you know how to play against them or how you can beat them, then they don't know what to do. Roger is the opposite. He is like a chess player. He reads the game unbelievable. If you play one system and he doesn't like it, then he plays so that you cannot play that system. So he's really great on court and he always has a great answer for however you play him."

Question: Is Roger the most difficult player that you have ever played against?

Rainer Schuettler: "Actually, for my game, I like the way Roger plays. Because it's a little bit the way I like it. But because Rafa, for me, is more tough with high spins to my backhand, he's lefty so he always has great angles. So I think Roger has a lot of difficulty with him because he hits a million balls high to his backhand with a big angle. And it's just hard on him. You have to move well. You have to hit the ball perfectly. You have to get back into position on the court. And so, for me, what can you say about Roger? One of the greatest players ever. Of course it's difficult to beat him. But from game systems-wise, Rafa was a little bit tougher for me because he's lefty and high spins to my backhand was never my strength."

Question: When you saw Roger play early on, did you imagine he would become so great as he did?

Rainer Schuettler: "You always can see a young guy with talent. But many things can happen with the pros. Injuries. I saw a lot who were No. 1 juniors in the world. But then something happened, injuries, or they never really made it through. And you could see if he's healthy and he continues to practice well, to stay so close to the game, that he tries to improve, that he will be an unbelievable player."

1999 Toulouse R32 Federer 6-7 1-6
2000 Milan R32   Federer 3-6 4-6
2002 Australian Open R32 Federer 6-7 6-7 4-6
2002 Dubai R16 Schuettler 6-3 6-1

"It's an experience you can't buy."

Peter Luczak: "I guess I was pretty lucky to get to play him in my career. It was first round at the French Open in I think 2010. At the time I was a bit unlucky to draw him in the first round. I had Nadal in the first round at the Aussie Open, the next slam I had Federer in the first round. It was pretty special to play on the center court though, against one of the best players of all time, arguably the best ever. I was pretty nervous, obviously. I got off to a good start, it was 4-all in the first set, then he just started working you out. It was 6-4. Second set 6-1 and third set 6-2 or 6-3. But it's an experience you can't buy. If I had played against a lesser player I might have won one match and probably would have ended up losing second or third round. If you get that experience to play Roger, now that I've played him, it's a pretty big privilege and honor."

Question: Were you pleased with how you played?

Peter Luczak: "Yeah, I was. You know, he's one of the greats so I didn't really expect to win. I played pretty well. I played as well as I could I think. Obviously he was too good for me."

Question: Is Federer the best you ever played? The hardest player to play against?

Peter Luczak: "It's...probably...it's tough to say. I only played him one time. if I'd played him maybe ten times maybe I could say. I just remember on another occasion I played Nalbandian and just felt helpess out there. He had a good day that day. And just the way he hit the ball, I felt really lucky to get those four games. I'd say Federer was one of the toughest to play. I played him on his least favorite surface, as well, on the clay. If I played him on hard court or grass it would probably be another story as well."

Question: Can you share a lasting memory of Roger, which sort of captures his essence, on the court or off the court?

Peter Luczak: "I was lucky to be a part of the Player Council for four years. I had two terms and he was on the Player Council as well. We're in the group meetings every couple of months. He and I got on quite well. I mean, we're pretty lucky and privileged to have him at the top of our sport because he's such a great guy. So down to earth. He really does care about all the players and the greater good of tennis. Whenever we were talking about topics or subjects he really had everything in mind, in consideration. He wants the game to be better and to improve. He cares about the lesser guys ranked 100, 1,000, whatever the case may be. So he wasn't just caring about the top guys. I think that's a lasting memory. That he's a really down to earth, good sort of bloke."

Question: Can you say there's anything you dislike about him?

Peter Luczak: "No. I can't say anything bad about Roger. He's a great guy. We're lucky to have him."

2010 Roland Garros R128 Federer 4-6 1-6 2-6

"He plays so happy."

Paul Capdeville: "Unbelievable feeling. Because I lost to him the year he lost two or three matches all the year. I feel so nervous in the beginning, I think I don't want to lose too easily. And then I play really well. I lost in three sets but - 2-4-4 - and the second and third set I was up 4-1 and 3-1. I had chances in both sets."

Question: Where?

Paul Capdeville: "U.S. Open. I play unbelievable. I try my best shots on every point. Roger makes it look so easy with good shots. He's an unbelievable player."

Question: Can you share a lasting memory of Roger, on the court or off?

Paul Capdeville: "I think it's when the match is done, he's in the locker room with friends, so happy and screaming in the locker room. I think he's a player, he plays so happy, I think."

2007 U.S. Open R64 Federer 1-6 4-6 4-6

"He's an extraordinary tennis player on the outside and inside of him he's still the normal guy."

Ilija Bozoljac: "I was really happy that I'm actually going to get to play the biggest tennis player alive. In the beginning I was kind of anxious about it. And I felt a little scared. But that was for just a couple of minutes. After I hit a couple of balls with him I felt great. I have to say it was really an honor for me to stand there and play against Roger and to play that way - I lost in four close sets. And I had a few chances. I mean, I enjoyed every point. It doesn't matter that I lost. I enjoyed the whole match."

Question: Were you happy with your performance?

Ilija Bozoljac: "I was. You're never completely happy when you lose a match. I was playing, I think, on a good level. And I was able to play on the same level as he was, maybe a little bit less. But I had chances but I didn't really take all my chances and I cannot be fully happy with that achievement. If you lose, it doesn't matter against who you play, when you step on the court against each other your goal is to win. I was really trying to win that match. I wasn't able. But I gave my best there. And hopefully next time I play him I'll try to give a little bit more and maybe win."

Question: After you won the set you must have thought to yourself: Hey, I can win this thing now.

Ilija Bozoljac: "When you're on the tennis court you don't think about winning or losing. You just think through the whole match just to play well and to be focused and to fight for every point. That's how I felt. In the beginning, the first game, I was like: Oh my God, I'm playing Roger! But after that I was just trying to play my game, focusing on myself, not much about the opponent, that time it was Roger. I managed to have some chances but I lost them. People would think it's so much different to play a player like this than to play some other player, regular player. But I felt even better. I felt like every point that he makes or I make, it was just so enjoyable. I loved it."

Question: Was Federer the hardest player for you to play?

Ilija Bozoljac: "For sure toughest to beat. But to play, I would say not. The way he constructs the points, how he plays is really nice to watch. Like you are watching a ballerina. You want to clap every time he makes a point. Because this is actually the game the guy is playing I think technically the best game that you can possibly play. We guys, other players appreciate it. So it was really an honor."

Question: Lasting memory of Roger, on court or off?

Ilija Bozoljac: "I knew him before I played. And I played him in doubles in Davis Cup against Switzerland. We lost three tough sets Zimo (Nenad Zimonjic) and I. It was 7-6, 4 and 4. But I played him before in the court so I knew how he was. And I have to say he's a great player and a great guy off the court as well. And I think that makes an even bigger picture of him. Nice guy. I just appreciate everything I have with him, on the court and outside of the court. And thank him for that. What is really, for me, surprising, the top guy like this, Roger, he often, when he sees me at a Grand Slam, he asks me like how I did, I play qualies, how did the match go, little questions like this. He just really wants to know what's going on. And he's really, really nice. He has good interaction with the other players. And my personal feeling is he's just an extraordinary tennis player on the outside and inside of him he's still the normal guy. Like he hasn't changed much but he's just an extraordinary tennis player."

2010 Wimbledon R64 Federer 3-6 7-6 4-6 6-7

"When you practice with Roger Federer you don't want to be late, right?"

Benjamin Becker: "The first time I played Roger was in 2006 which was my first year in professional tennis, my second year, but my first year on the Tour. And yeah, it was tough, when you know you're going to play him you know it's a tough task ahead of you. So for me, first it was an honor to be on the court. You don't really believe you can win, to have a chance, just try to look good. Then I played him a couple of years later and it changed a little bit. Obviously you go on court and try to beat him. So then you're more settled into the Tour. You know, maybe someday you can beat him if you have one of your best days. But I never got to beat him. I broke him a couple of times. I played him one 7-6 in one tiebreak but he's just too good, just too many things on the court that keep you off your balance. And it's tough to compete with him."

Question: What is your most memorable match with Federer?

Benjamin Becker: "I think the first one because the first one is always special. The first one you just come up to the Tour, you follow all those guys and all the sudden you compete against them. It's kind of special. I remember I played him - I wasn't really on court, I was more like looking around and try to not look at him. And not get taken away in the moment. The first was special. I mean, all of them are special. Once you have a chance to compete against him and know what you had against it, it's good. It's a good challenge. It's why we're out here - to have good challenges. The last one I played was in 2012 in his hometown of Basel which was also fun because it was full stadium, great atmosphere and it was a close match. Until after like the middle of the second set, then he just took off. And won the last four games in a row I think. So yeah, most of them are special."

Question: Looking back, how do you feel you performed against him?

Benjamin Becker: "The first one I didn't perform well. It was too soon, I couldn't play my game. He broke me once every set and I couldn't get his return back. The second one we had a close second set. It was Madrid on clay. I had some chances in the tiebreak. He played well. The last one we did, we had a tight first set and I was up a break in the second. It's always a good start of winning a set to break him. I think the last one I played was probably my best against him. I had some chances. When I was up a break I was maybe a little too passive. But that happens though."

Question: Lasting memory on or off court about Roger Federer?

Benjamin Becker: "He's just overall a very nice guy. We speak German to each other. So obviously he can speak out native language but he speaks three or four languages anyway. He's a very nice guy. He always comes, says hi. He always knows what you dld In the results. So he follows the tournaments. You know, when I just came up, he knew that I already won a few Challengers before. To me it was pretty surprising. But that's how he is, he follows tennis. He looks at every guy, he really does his homework. He really does his preparation. And for him to be really nice, I mean, I warmed him up for his Australian Open tournament in '08 a couple of times. And then I left. And he wanted me still, 'Hey, can you still come and warm me up?' So it was pretty fun."

"Actually, also once, a memory, I was late for practice. When you practice with Roger Federer you don't want to be late, right? My coach told me we practice at 5 but he actually set it up for 4. So I'm preparing, I'm eating at 4:15 to get ready. And all the sudden my coach said, 'Hey, they're on court, they're waiting for you!' So you come a half hour, 45 minutes late for practice with Roger. He was very cool about it. He was playing some mini tennis soccer and he was just laughing, saying 'Don't worry about it, it's fine.' He's very relaxed. So on the side that he's also unbelievable, maybe the best tennis player ever - and he's also a nice person too."

2006 Tokyo   SF Federer 3-6 4-6
2010 Madrid Masters   R32 Federer 2-6 6-7
2012 Basel R32   Federer 5-7 3-6

"When it was close in the end he always came with his best shot."

Ivo Karlovic: "Well, right now it is not anymore unbelievable because I already played him many times."

Scoop: 11.

Ivo Karlovic: "Yeah so now it's like almost every week [smiles]. When it was our first match I was a little bit overwhelmed and I didn't play as well maybe. But after that I was always a little more relaxed and it was easier. But I only beat him once. But it was a lot of close matches."

Question: What was your most memorable match with Roger?

Ivo Karlovic: "The one I won in '08 in Cincinnati. It was definitely one of my best wins in my career."

Scoop: You came very close many times.

Ivo Karlovic: "Yeah. It was a lot of tiebreaks and everything. But when it was a close match in the end, he always came with his best shot."

40

Question: Is Roger the most difficult guy for you to play?

Ivo Karlovic: "Well, obviously because I only beat him once in all those matches. Obviously yeah. And of course he may be the best one ever."

Question: Can you share a lasting memory of Roger, on or off court?

Ivo Karlovic: "He was always really nice with me. Like always. Like even in the matches he was always correct and everything. Of course, for me, the best memories were when I beat him. For him maybe all the other matches [smiles]."

Question: Ever practice with him? Or have a conversation?

Ivo Karlovic: "Practice - no. In the locker room we had a little bit of interaction."

Question: Why is he so difficult to play?

Ivo Karlovic: "Number one, he's unbelievably fast, like unbelievable. And there's not really any bad shots, like any weaknesses in his game. You really have to play. Like me against him, I really have to play aggressive. But on the otherhand, he's unbelievably fast and his defense is unbelievable also. There is not a lot you can really do, only when it's your day, you can hit winners. But that is not happening every day so it's difficult."

Question: Do you remember what was especially working for you when you did beat him?

Ivo Karlovic: "I was hitting my forehands, every one, even if it's out or it's in. I wasn't missing a lot. And my kick serve was bouncing really high so he was having a lot of problems with it."

Question: Did he say anything to you after this match? Like, finally you got me.

Ivo Karlovic: "Only congratulations. Because that day after he lost his No. 1 spot. So I don't know if he was really happy about it [smiles]."

2004 Wimbledon R16 Federer 3-6 6-7 6-7
2004 Gstaad R16 Federer 6-7 3-6 6-7
2007 Montreal Masters R32 Federer 6-7 6-7
2007 Basel   SF Federer 6-7 6-7
2007 Paris Masters R32   Federer 3-6 6-4 3-6
2008 Rome Masters R16 Federer 6-7 3-6
2008 Cincinnati Masters R16 Karlovic 7-6 4-6 7-6
2009 Indian Wells Masters R32 Federer 6-7 3-6
2009 Rome Masters R32 Federer 4-6 3-6
2009 Wimbledon Q Federer 3-6 5-7 6-7

2012 Australian Open R32 Federer 6-7 5-7 3-6

"He's so easy to play. He's difficult to beat."

Teymuraz Gabashvili: "Actually it was my first Wimbledon main draw I think, or second. Center court. So for me it was not because it was Roger Federer, for me it was center court of Wimbledon one of the most prestigious courts for all tennis players, like the biggest in history. It was such a feeling of something special because first day, full stadium, a lot of crowd. I played before in front of a big crowd - against James Blake at U.S. Open also center court, biggest in the world. But it was a different feeling, Wimbledon is a classical tennis tournament for the world wide. Of course it's a special feeling a little bit more because it was with Roger Federer. I think that year we played he already won it four or five times so it was nice, it was nice. I remember I slipped and fell down in the first game or second and commentator Boris Becker was laughing about it."

Question: You could hear him commentating while on the court playing?

Teymuraz Gabashvili: "No, when I was watching a tape of the match. It was actually a good time for me but it was a bad draw for me, I was playing good. To play Roger Federer is not a good draw [smiles]."

Question: How do you feel about your performance against Roger that day?

Teymuraz Gabashvili: "Ups and downs because first set was quite easy. We start at 1-all, then he broke, broke me again. It was 6-1 first set. Then it was a little bit more of a fight. Third set I had a couple break point chances I think. I remember I was really close to coming back in the set but I couldn't do it. But the first set I just gave up because of nerves and, you know, I feel nervous going into the court and I felt that he played pretty relaxed. And he could come up higher but also it's first match for him and anything can happen. And so if I break him back in the third set he would get nervous and he wouldn't feel comfortable. Yeah, I think it was a good match to watch for the crowd, I enjoyed it."

Question: Why is Federer so difficult to play do you think?

Teymuraz Gabashvili: "He's so easy to play. He's difficult to beat [smiles]. You know? For example, it's much more difficult to play Rafa because he doesn't give you any points. Just fight, fight for every ball. Not like Roger, if he feels comfortable score he can, you know, doesn't run to a ball. Of course, he knows when it's time to make an ace. But the difference I felt that he had such unbelievable touch, couple of times he did serve and volley and I actually return pretty well, I remember he made unbelievable half-volley drop shots that I never saw it before. I showed a couple of guys, Yeah, only Federer can do this ball, you know? I felt like it was my point but the ball goes back two centimeters on my side. This was different, amazing."

Question: Do you have any relations with Federer off court?

Teymuraz Gabashvili: "For the biggest champions, no, with Nadal it's more friendly than with other guys. But Federer is much older than me, I think four or five more. Federer, he is different, so only hello and goodbeye and how are you pretty much. Not like friendship."

Question: Lasting memory of Roger, on or off court?

Teymuraz Gabashvili: "He has a pretty simple image. The same image always since he became No. 1, the classical player. The same image that he makes on the court you can feel he's very, very confident. Very, very confident. And only the biggest champions can be like this. I feel playing Rafa at Roland Garros was pretty much the same feeling. He kind of knew it's his home. I think Roger is like the greatest player ever, his results show it. Unfortunately I only played him once but I wish I play him more. Still I have chance. So we'll see [smiles]."

2007 Wimbledon R128 Federer 3-6 2-6 4-6

"The guy's been nothing short of really, really nice and really caring for some of the guys."

Somdev Devvarman: "It was definitely a surreal moment because before the match we were both in the trainer's room. It was in Dubai. Before the match we were both in the trainer's room getting taped and stretched out and all that good stuff. And he came very casual and very nice. So obviously, going in to the match you have a lot of respect for the guy, it goes without saying, for all his accomplishments, also I think for the kind of person he is and what he's done for tennis, off the court, the way he carries himself also. There's so many things that go into it. Obviously you admire the guy so when you walk on it's a little different than to walk on for another tennis match."

"I think he made it a lot easier. He's always smiling, he's always nice to you. He's very laid back, very relaxed. And it was a surreal feeling. Like I said, when I walked on the court, it was in Dubai, there actually happened to be a lot of Indians as well. So it was a nice feeling to go out there, play Roger, have a fair crowd that was cheering for both of us. It was first round. It was a fantastic experience. And ever since the guy's always been nice to me and he's always helped support anything I've asked him for, signatures for a charity event and everything else. The guy's been nothing short of really, really nice and really caring for some of the guys. And is a class act all the way through."

Question: Did anything surprise you about being on the court with him? How he played?

Somdev Devvarman: "No, other than how good he really was [smiles]. Obviously, on TV you see certain things but actually being on the other side of the net you feel pressure in so many different ways, the way he plays. So, yeah, it was a great experience overall."

Question: How do you feel you performed in this match?

Somdev Devvarman: "Actually, okay. Obviously, I had some chances. I had maybe one look on his serve, or two. Two deuces on his serve. And break points. But other than that, nothing else. I think I played pretty well. I competed hard, gave it my best. That's kind of the way I play, just go out there, try my hardest against everybody and leave it all out there. So I did that again. The guy obviously was too good and served too well."

Question: Lasting memory or anecdote, on or off court, something that captures his essence?

Somdev Devvarman: "The next day we came out, I was in the locker room, so I told him, I said, Listen, if you want to warm up or a practice, let me know. And he's like, Yeah, actually tomorrow. So I went out there and we started talking about just a lot of random things. The guy's intelligent, there's no question. One of the things we talked about was cricket, which was surprising that he knew anything about because he's Swiss. And he knew a lot about Dubai. And I know quite a lot about it too. We talked a little bit about it. It was funny, because he was a little late, he was apologetic. He said the twins were sick and he had to take care of them. It was just kind of funny for me to be like wow, so this guy's a normal guy, he's taking care of his kids and coming over here. And he's so laid back before the match. He's a talkative guy if you know him. I don't know him that well. From what I've seen, he's a talkative, friendly guy."

2011 Dubai R32 Federer 3-6 3-6
2013 French Open R64 Federer 2-6 1-6 1-6

"Every single ball that is not perfect he takes advantage of it."

Andrei Pavel: "Well, the first time I play him I have a pretty good feeling because I won [laughs]. That was the only time I ever won against him. I played him like three or four times in a matter of three months exactly when he was No. 1. He's been No. 1 for a long time. It's a feeling like sometimes even if you play your best you ever have to raise your game a lot of times. And that's when the mistake comes. And when he's on fire there's just a feeling like that he doesn't give you any chances. Every single ball that is not perfect he takes advantage of it. And he's so relaxed and so confident on the court. A lot of times if you're not fully solid and play your best game, he just blows you away."

Question: Was Federer the most difficult player for you to play in your career?

Andrei Pavel: "No, he was the best one but not the most difficult. Guys like Santoro, Karlovic - it's hard to enjoy playing against them. Their games are so different than everybody else. But no, Federer is the best, he's not the most difficult but he's the best guy."

Question: Your most memorable match with Federer?

Andrei Pavel: "Well, I had a couple of them. I had a match in Davis Cup against him which I think was pretty good. I still lost in three sets but it was a good match. I had a match in Dubai or Rotterdam I think that I should have won there but you can see why he's been No. 1 for so long. On big points he came out with huge shots or he made me play unbelievable, difficult shots."

Question: Lasting memory of Roger, on or off court?

Andrei Pavel: "Well, I think Roger is one of the coolest guys. He's really relaxed, he's really polite, very friendly with everybody. He didn't change in any way his personality. And I think that's a plus-point."

2000 Hamburg Masters R64 Pavel 6-4 6-3
2000 Basel   R16 Federer 6-7 4-6
2001 Rotterdam   SF Federer 7-6 4-6 0-6
2002 Miami Masters Q Federer 1-6 1-6
2004 Davis Cup   Federer 3-6 2-6 5-7
2004 Rotterdam   R16 Federer 6-7 5-7
2004 Dubai   Q Federer 3-6 2-6
2004 Indian Wells Masters   R64 Federer 1-6 1-6
2004 U.S. Open R16   Federer walkover

Chapter 4 Roger Federer Faces The Media

How many interviews has Roger Federer done during his career? Perhaps over 5,000, maybe 10,000. After every match Federer, who can speak five different languages, will give press conferences in primarily English, French, and German, answering approximately ten to twenty questions from print, radio, TV and digital journalists. Then he will do more radio and TV interviews.

Federer is so in-demand that major magazine requests for a one-on-one interview can take several months to arrange, if they are accepted. As the "Face of Tennis", Federer has been a media magnet for a decade now, parrying newsmen and women with grace and aplomb, as easily as if they were probing shots from opponents and practice partners.

Fortunately, I was able to do a one-on-one interview with Federer in 1999. Roger was still largely unknown by the sports world back then, just in his second year as pro. At the 1999 U.S. Open qualifying tournament in late August, I went in search of and found young Roger sitting at his locker alone after he won his first match. He agreed to do a spontaneous interview. Here is the Biofile interview we did that weekday afternoon.

Question: Who were your childhood heroes?

Federer: "Edberg. Becker. Sampras."

Question: Ever tell Sampras he was a hero of yours?

Federer: "I won't go up to him and say 'I like your game.' You can't say it. I never talked to him. Now that I play against him, can't have idols anymore. Just like to see him play."

Question: Do you have any nicknames?

Federer: "Rogie."

Question: Hobbies and interests?

Federer: "Sports in general, cinema, friends, all that kind of stuff."

Question: What has been the greatest moment of your career so far?

Federer: "I've got a few actually [smiles]. Orange Bowl - that brought me to No. 1 junior in the world. Winning junior Wimbledon ('98). The victory over Carlos Moya (in Marseille, France on ATP Tour). The victory in the Davis Cup (vs. Davide Sanguinetti). My biggest wins."

Question: Your most painful moment?

Federer: "Last few weeks. Didn't play very well. I was very down. After this match (a 6-4, 6-4 win over Edwin Kempes in the first round of U.S. Open qualifying) I feel much better."

       ***

[Note: Federer entered the 1999 U.S. Open in a slump. His previous results in the summer of 1999 were:

Queens - lost to Byron Black 3-6, 0-6

Wimbledon - lost to Jiri Novak 3-6, 6-3, 6-4, 3-6, 4-6

Gstaad - lost to Younes El Aynaoui 2-6, 3-6

Davis Cup in Belgium - lost to Christophe Van Garsse 6-7, 6-3, 6-1, 5-7, 1-6 and lost to Xavier Malisse 6-4, 3-6, 5-7, 6-7

Segovia Challenger - beat Quino Munoz 7-6, 6-4, lost to Nicolas Escude 6-3, 1-6, 4-6

Washington, DC - lost to Bjorn Phau 2-6, 3-6

Long Island qualifying draw - beat Todd Meringoff 6-2, 3-6, 6-3
 and lost to Eric Taino 2-6, 2-6

U.S. Open qualifying draw - beat Edwin Kempes 6-4, 6-4
 and lost to Ivo Heuberger 6-7, 2-6.]

    ***

Question: Your pre-match feeling, how do you feel before a match?

Federer: "As always, before an important match, always very nervous. It's a good feeling. It shows I think that match is very important for me. After match, relax. In the beginning you hope you just play okay. Which is, start to play, get the rhythm and everything. And after two, three games you're not nervous anymore. Night before, go out to eat with friends, eat pasta, drink a lot of water before."

Question: Your favorite movies?

Federer: "Good Will Hunting. Entrapment. Enemy Of The State."

Question: Your favorite music?

Federer: "Anything on top of the charts all over the world."

Question: Favorite meal?

Federer: "Gnocchi Gorgonzola."

Question: Favorite breakfast cereal?

Federer: "Rice Crispies [laughs]."

Question: Favorite ice cream flavor?

Federer: "Strawberry."

Question: Who are some favorite athletes you like to watch?

Federer: "Michael Jordan. Sampras. Hingis. (Why her?) I mean, she's the best. Lennox Lewis. (What about him?) The best. He's big and strong and he should have got the win against Holyfield [Note: The judges of their March 1999 match in New York City controversially ruled it a draw.] (Sammy) Sosa, (Mark) McGwire. Eric Lindros. Peter Forsberg. More and more hockey. American football was not too interesting to me. Too many breaks in the action. Plus I don't understand the rules too good [smiles]. Marcelo Rios. (Why him? Did you ever tell him?) I like his game. We don't talk. Because he never talks to anybody [laughs]. I just like his game. He's fun to watch because he's a different type of guy."

Question: First car?

Federer: "Haven't got a car. Can't have till I'm 19. I guess I'll have an Opel."

Question: Funny tennis memory, anything from tennis that made you laugh?

Federer: "I was playing a friend Marco when I was 14. Playing in Basel. And it was like six o'clock. And this bird just goes on the net [smiles]. My friend - he didn't see the bird and he starts serving. And he serves and the little bird - BOOM! Right on the body. The bird came to my side of the net. And it was on the ground, like, shaking, then Boom, dead. Feathers all over the court. He didn't know what happened. I'm like, 'Stop! Stop! There's a bird on the net!' And he goes Boom and just hits it. That was unbelievable."

Question: An early tennis memory, any kind of early memory from tennis?

Federer: "I remember always loving to play against the cupboards, against the doors at home. With any kind of ball...soft ball, tennis ball. My mom always got upset at me, because, Bang, bang, bang!, all day long [smiles]."

Question: Closest friends from tennis?

Federer: "Marc Rosset - he helps me. George Bastl. Ivo Heuberger. All the Swiss players. A few French players. The Moroccans - Karim Alami, Hicham Arazi, Younes El Aynaoui - are also very nice."

Question: People qualities most admired?

Federer: "That they smile a lot. Friendly. Helpful. And I dont like, I don't like it when somebody lies. Because I never lie."

Question: What were some of your childhood dreams?

Federer: "Always had tennis in my mind. Tennis was my dream. I just hope that I always be healthy and not injured."

Here is a sampling of some of Federer's various interviews throughout different stages of his career.

July 2, 2001 after beating Pete Sampras in five sets at Wimbledon.

Q. You just changed the course of history, stopped a 32-match winning streak that Pete Sampras had. How does that feel?

Roger Federer: It feels unbelievable, of course. I mean, I went out on the court today trying to beat him. I mean, I knew it was not going to be easy. I'm very happy about my performance today, from the first to the last point. Yeah, at the end, it's just a great feeling I've never had before.

Q. Where do you think you won this match? In the return?

Roger Federer: Yeah, I would say returns because I had the feeling I had more chances than he did . Especially in the first three sets, I always had chances to break him. But he came up with some big serves. Then suddenly in the fourth and in the fifth, I didn't have any break chances anymore. He was just like serving too good. Maybe I was a little bit passive on the returns. But, I don't know, I'm still happy with my game.

Q. You never seemed to lose your composure out there, no matter what. Was that a big factor for you?

Roger Federer: Yeah, I mean, I felt good, actually, from the start, as I won my first service game. I think the first service game is never easy, especially for me the first time coming out on Centre Court, playing Pete Sampras, one of my former idols. Then, I don't know, I won it I think love or 15. That gave me a little boost to go into the match. The whole court was packed. There's no way you're going to quit, I guess.

Q. Was it difficult to not think of him as your idol? When did he become your "former idol"?

Roger Federer: Well, sometimes it was weird, you know, I look on the other side of the net, I saw him, sometimes I was like, it's just true, you know, kind of that this is happening now, that I'm playing against him. But then it just goes away, this feeling. You think about your serve, where you're going to go, then it's like playing against maybe some other player, you know. But obviously something special for me to play Pete.

Q. How did you stay so calm, particularly after you'd been ahead twice? How did you stay so calm?

Roger Federer: Well, I had the feeling that that first set was very important, that I came back from set point down to win the set. That gave me a lot of confidence for the rest because I had the feeling, I mean, I really can beat him. I had that feeling all the way. That's probably why I won today. I had played a bad game there in the second to lose the set. I mean, I had problems with my leg. That probably relaxed me mentally a bit. I mean, I had trouble running to a couple balls. But I was totally relaxed. That's why I was not tired in the fifth. I felt good really all five sets.

Q. He's the king of grass. Why did you think you could beat him? What was it about his game?

Roger Federer: I mean, in the beginning his serve was just massive. I had no chance. I mean, normally I'm pretty good in reading serves. I just had no chance. Especially, I mean, his second serve was as fast as my first serve (smiling). You think, "How is that possible?" But I still had the feeling I had a good chance on his second serve, even though he was serving 120 miles per hour. Suddenly when I had Love-40, 15-40 a few times on his serve, so I knew I will always get a chance in the match. I was holding also serves pretty easy at that time. I mean, I don't know why I had that feeling today. A lot of friends and players told me, "This year I think you can really beat him." I've played a great year so far - better than he did.

Q. What have you done to improve your game this year?

Roger Federer: This year? Physically, I feel much better. Big points. I mean, I've been playing unbelievable, especially on breakpoints against me, I've been saving so many breakpoints. My serve has improved. On the grass I can serve and volley now. Before, I couldn't do that now.

Q. Were you saying in the locker room there were a lot of players saying he was beatable? Is that the view that's been held?

Roger Federer: A few players, a few coaches, my friends, myself. I knew I had a chance. But, of course, I was not like a hundred percent. I mean, he's the man on grass.

Q. How did you feel after that fourth set tiebreaker? Were you concerned at that point?

Roger Federer: What really worried me was that volley I missed at 1-All. After the return, I thought, "What happened?" I looked kind of to him, missed a volley. From then on, it was just his tiebreaker. I mean, I felt good already going into the tiebreaker because I know if I lose this tiebreaker, I can go in the fifth set, no problem for me, because I was feeling good physically at the time.

Q. You weren't worried in the fifth set about losing?

Roger Federer: When I was down two breakpoints, I was very worried because I had the feeling he was raising his game, started making the returns, making me play. There I was very scared for a while. But I survived it and came back strong.

Q. Do you think you have a real chance of winning the title now?

Roger Federer: I think this match will give me as much confidence as I can get. This is my biggest win in my life. Now I'm going to play Henman or Martin, if that's correct. I've played them before. Never beat Henman. I beat Martin. I have to look really match per match. After beating Pete, I think maybe I have a chance. I don't know.

Q. Pete said when he played you today, seemed like sometimes he felt like he was playing himself because you don't show a lot on the court, don't show a lot of emotion. I know you saw him as a kid. Did you pattern your behavior on the court after Pete?

Roger Federer: Not at all actually. I mean, I was throwing around my racquet like you probably don't imagine. Helicopters were flying all over (laughter). I mean, I was getting kicked out of practice sessions non-stop when I was 16. Now since maybe I think this year, I started just to relax a little bit more on court. I'm not smashing as many racquets as before.

Q. What changed it? Why suddenly did you decide to do it?

Roger Federer: I don't know if I grew up a little bit. I realized that the racquet throwing didn't help my game because I was always getting very negative. I used to talk also much more. Now, I mean, I don't talk anymore. I'm just positive, you know. Also, of course, to play Centre Court in front of a packed crowd, to play Pete Sampras, I don't know, doesn't make you scream, you know, throw racquets. I think that's pretty normal.

Q. You've been kicking the butt of us Americans all season. In our country, we have lots of nice mountains, lots of tennis courts. What can we possibly do to get you to jump ship and come to America?

Roger Federer: I don't know. It's tough to say. I mean, it's true, I played unbelievable Davis Cup tie there against you guys. Today again I played great. Actually, I was thinking about the Davis Cup during today's match because I thought Pete could also have came to the Davis Cup tie, I maybe would have beat him also (laughter). I mean, I don't know.

Q. Sound pretty confident.

Roger Federer: Too confident, I think (smiling).

Q. What did Pete say to you after the game? Did you have a chance to talk?

Roger Federer: I think he just congratulate me when we shook hands. Otherwise, I mean, he was on one side of the locker, I was on the other side. I think he was very disappointed, I mean, obviously after such a loss. I don't know. We didn't speak at all, actually.

Q. Were you aware that Pete had never lost a five-set match at Wimbledon? When you got into the fifth set, not wrapping it up in four, did you have any concern that this is where Pete Sampras is the master, in the fifth set?

Roger Federer: I actually didn't know his record of five sets. I don't know why, what it was, but I had the feeling that in five sets, I was really good. I don't know if the record is the same. I felt like in five sets, I'm really good. I heard about it. His five-set record, he was probably like 70% he wins them, five sets. I heard that when he played Barry Cowan. I told myself, "Yeah, but he has lost five-setters, so I think I can really do it today, as well."

Q. When you saw him struggle with Barry Cowan, had that in the back of your mind, did that change your feeling about him on grass?

Roger Federer: I mean, at that time I was also in the second round or third round maybe.

Q. Once you were getting ready to play him, you had that Cowan match in the back of your mind.

Roger Federer: I was just happy that Barry Cowan took him to five sets. That showed a little bit that he wasn't playing his best on grass probably. I mean, a normal Pete Sampras would beat him in three. He just lost the tiebreak in the third. Probably gave me a little bit of good feeling inside, you know, that I can also myself push him to five sets maybe.

Q. The injury you have?

Roger Federer: It's on the adductor.

Q. 4-All, first breakpoint, he hits the return low to you, are you thinking you're going to win the match at that point?

Roger Federer: 4-All, what was it?

Q. In the fifth set.

Roger Federer: The half volley I played, yeah, I was. I was scared when I had to face breakpoint. I just told myself, "Be aggressive, go to the net." Yeah, I came up with a good half volley, finished it on the backhand side. I think where I was a little bit scared was on the other breakpoint, that second serve, played it to his forehand. He had a running forehand. When he hits it, his ball stays hit on the forehand side. I was happy he didn't make it.

Q. Could you tell us a little bit about how you developed in Switzerland? Was tennis always your game?

Roger Federer: I started playing at the age of three. I was playing soccer at the same time. At like 10 or 12-years-old, I had to make a decision what I'm going to do now more than the other one. I had more success in tennis. Decided at 14 to go down to the National Tennis Center, but it was in the French-speaking part of Switzerland, I'm coming from the German. For me, it was very tough the first half of year. I wanted to go home. I was not happy. I was crying when I have to leave on Sunday. Then I went to the Orange Bowl, under 14. Came back, felt good, started to win matches. At 16, the tennis center changed to the part of Switzerland where they speak both languages. For the future, they can go in French-speaking schools and German. I decided to quit school at that time, at 16, because I felt like school was bothering me from my best tennis. I quit school and just went (showing upward movement with his hand) very quickly. I won a junior tournament and finished No. 1 in Juniors then. Also the change from Juniors to pros was not as tough.

Q. What is he missing from his game that he had two years ago? Obviously he's still a great player. Has he come down a level?

Roger Federer: I don't know. I mean, I was very surprised that he was serve-volleying at the French Open first and second serve. It looks like he's not ready to stay back and rally from the baseline. I agree, it's not his game. But somewhere you have to, I mean, stay back or play a little bit more passive. I don't know. He's got his one game now, serve and volley first and second serve. I don't know if he was doing that two years ago.

Interview at U.S. Open August 30, 2006.

The hard work has all paid off so far, you know, and now I'm always in the position where I'm the big, big favorite for every tournament I play. That, obviously, has been tough sometimes for other players.

Q. You seem to handle that stoically. It has to be a tremendous amount of pressure.

Roger Federer: It depends how you look at it, you know. I say I always prefer to be the favorite than the underdog. That's definitely worked out for me since I became No. 1. I never lost that spot and never looked back. That gave me more confidence than pressure really.

Q. Are you enjoying your tennis career more now than you ever have?

Roger Federer: It's totally different now to the beginning. In the beginning you're trying to feel your way into the Tour, trying to look for friends, trying to understand the way it runs. You know, trying to get to know the center courts, the fans, how does the whole thing work.

By the time you find out, you know, you're in the early 20s, and then the pressure builds up on you, you know. Through the media, they want you to have results and everything, so you're more thinking about these kind of things.

Whereas now, I really concentrate on how I need to get ready for a tournament. I know exactly what to expect. So it's a whole lot easier now than it used to be.

Q. You spoke a moment ago of times when you played extraordinarily well. At that moment when it's all coming together, can you describe that? Is there a feeling of lightness? Is there a feeling of joy? Is everything effortless? Can you try and share with us what that moment is like when you're playing like that.

Roger Federer: No, I guess it's just a feeling you get inside, you know, every time you have a chance to attack, you never lose a point. In defense, you believe in your capabilities of coming up with a great shot at the right time. Big points, you know you're gonna serve well.

You have a feeling in the baseline rallies that everything is slowed down for you and for the other guy it's quicker, you know. Feelings like this then make you just play fantastic tennis.

August 18, 2012 after beating Novak Djokovic 6-0 7-6 in the Cincinnati Masters Series final. Interview on court with CBS TV's Mary Jo Fernandez:

Question: Roger do you ever recall a time where you've gone through a tournament and not dropped serve the entire time?

Roger Federer: "Maybe once. In Qatar years ago. I wouldn't even be sure anymore. I have a few titles, so it could have happened. But it's a rare thing, very rare. I couldn't be more happy. Especially coming through in the final against a guy like Djokovic who had an amazing run all year. And he's so tough on hard courts. I really expected myself to be broken, of course, I actually announced it yesterday, 'Someone will get broken for sure.' I thought it was gonna be me but it didn't happen. It's almost amazing."

Question: You're playing against probably the best returner in the game, so do you approach your serve game any differently when you face Novak?

Roger Federer: "Yeah you do. You just feel more pressure on the first serve. Because you feel if you double fault in any game, you're probably gonna get broke. Sort of love-15, or love-30, you have 50% chance to get broken. So those stats kind of creep into your mind. And kind of have a big effect how you play your baseline points. But I was able to get a quick start, particularly in the first set. Then the second set, maybe I didn't serve that great anymore. I had good variation and played aggressive from the baseline. And maybe Novak never really got comfortable."

Question: At the start of the season you talked about some of your goals, wanting to reclaim the No. 1 ranking, which you have, winning another grand slam, which you did. You got the silver at the Olympics. How do you re-set? Like what do you look forward to now in your career which has been so long?

Roger Federer: "Well, maybe it's a, I think it's a great stepping-stone to what's coming hopefully, because I didn't have a top final in the Olympics. I definitely didn't want that to happen to me again where I lose nine games off the charts and then end up being crushed in the final. Eventhough I didn't feel that way but it wasn't a great final of mine. I'm happy I bounced back here, right away, won a title. Eventhough I just achieved all the goals you just said - I wanted to win Wimbledon again. I wanted to become World No. 1 again. So there could be a letdown. But I didn't show it, yet [smiles]. I hope it's not gonna happen [chuckles a bit]. We'll see how New York goes. All this, I couldn't feel better right now in terms of confidence. But also the body's holding up well. The year is still very long. I hope I can play really well in the next couple of weeks."

Question: Novak said he's probably gonna take a few days off to recover. What will you do to prepare for the U.S. Open?

Roger Federer: "I'll take a couple of days off. Then I'll start practicing in New York. And over there we obviously have a lot of media requests and sponsor requests. And then friends I want to catch up with. Spend time with family. And just settle down in New York, you know, get used to the craziness in New York. I'm just so looking forward to it. Yeah, it's exciting time ahead of us and it's just a good time of year, this one."

Question: Well, congratulations on winning your 21st Masters Series and good luck in New York.

Roger Federer: "Thank you very much."

Roger Federer Interview at 2012 US Open after beating Fernando Verdasco in

three sets.

Q. 26 out of 27 net points won today. Do you ever remember a statistic like that?

Roger Federer: I had no clue my stats were that good coming in. Fernando did have some good chances for good passing shots. Looking back, I don't remember missing too many volleys and overheads, all that stuff. Probably half the time I didn't have to volley because it was hard to hit a good pass. It was windy. Usually when I do come in, it's probably on one I can be very offensive on. But I really tried to play offensive against Bjorn Phau in my second match. I did lose more points than I was hoping to. I think that gave me the confidence to move forward today and conditions helped that because it was quicker during the day.

Q. What are your thoughts on the Davis Cup tie against The Netherlands in Amsterdam? Will you be there?

Roger Federer: Probably take a decision soon. It's obviously one that's an interesting choice of surface from their side, playing outdoors on clay. But then again, you know, it's an exciting tie because Dutch fans are always amazing. I remember when I played there 2004 maybe, I'm not sure how long ago it was, 2003 I think it was, we had a great time. I hope obviously the Swiss can win. But it's going to be difficult. Away ties in Holland are always very difficult.

Q. But will you be there?

Roger Federer: Don't know yet. Take a decision next 10 days. A lot is happening in my life.

Q. The Spanish media published today that Rafael Nadal may not play until next year. How do you feel about it? Did you ever have a conversation with him about his many injuries?

Roger Federer: No.

Q. Maybe gave him some advice?

Roger Federer: No, we never really spoke about it, even though we see each other. He sees me taped up. I see him getting taped up. We see each other warming up for matches and so forth. You never really talk about that. I think it's quite personal except if one guy goes up to the other. But we're both very open and honest, you know. When I ask him how he's feeling, he's not feeling well, he'll tell me, I'm tired, a little injured. There's no real secrets out there because he knows and I know when we tell each other that stuff it doesn't leave the room. That's a nice relationship I have with Rafa. It's based on a lot of trust. So it's obviously not great news but one that was a possibility. So I'm not shocked about the news. I'm still hopeful that he'll be okay for the rest of the year.

Q. Aside from doing all these press conferences time and time again, what is the toughest thing you've had to go through in your career?

Roger Federer: It depends what 'tough' is. I don't know. I've had tough moments out there. I can't recall one. I've had so many nice ones that when it gets extremely tough, when you get tough questions, tough trips, tough matches, whatever that may be, you have to explain yourself, it's okay from time to time to have to go through that. You learn from it. You deal with it. You move on. You always try not to make the same mistake a few times. But it's happened to me, as well. Yeah, I can't recall a particular one.

Q. You're known for your game management. When you are having a tough time out on court, is the most important thing to stay calm?

Roger Federer: I mean, it is actually quite difficult. You're always in the limelight out on center court. That's almost every match for me now. There's no hiding spot out there. Doesn't matter how long you're out there for. Might be five hours. Basically the TV is just waiting for something to happen. It will not go unnoticed. I don't want to say you always have to be on your best behavior, but that can be tricky and difficult sometimes especially when you're younger because you're not quite aware of it yet. It's a very respectful game towards fans and your opponents and all that stuff. I'm happy it's that way. But obviously it's not always so easy to be composed about everything that goes on out there because we also have many emotions. We don't always feel great every day. When something is hurting or when you're sick, doesn't matter what it is, when you're trying not to show someone, it's tricky because they zoom in on you and you know that. You just try to go with it and you get used to it eventually.

Q. When you started out, social media is not what it is today. Is that better for a player to be able to tell people in their own words or is it better to be judged by the outside world?

Roger Federer: Well, I mean, yeah, it's true, social media didn't exist when I was coming along. I don't remember anyone doing it back then yet. Now it's got really big. Obviously now we have a lot of quick news, quick info, almost a bit too much for my liking at times. Sometimes you don't go in-depth any more. It's finding out a lot of information as quick as possible. You definitely have to get used to that as well. So the question was exactly? I'm a little slow, you see (smiling).

Q. From the athlete's standpoint, are you happier being able to give out the information yourself, or do you want other people to judge you?

Roger Federer: Well, I started using my website for that some time ago. Whenever I had an announcement to make, important, not important, at least it was a neutral platform. So none of the journalists would feel betrayed that I used one to announce. So I put it on the website and people did what they did. For me, the most important was that I could communicate with fans. The communication with the media happens for me here. I don't necessarily need social media to communicate more with you guys. I'm doing so much media all the time. For me, most important are the supporters and fans who travel the world with me. When I see them at practices or matches, this is when I want to interact with them. Of course, now there is this platform. Of course, from time to time I do write stuff, as well, but it's not my favorite thing to do. I do it because I know that the fans take pleasure. I don't actually post for anyone else but the supporters and the fans. People use it differently. I use it that way, still very casually, but it seems to work so far. We'll see how it goes in the future because things are changing.

Q. Stan said yesterday if you played more doubles you could be the best doubles player in the world. Do you think playing at the Olympics improved your singles game at all?

Roger Federer: I don't think so. But repeat yourself again. I just want to make sure I heard that.

Q. Has it improved your volley or your play at net? You played doubles four weeks ago at the Olympics...

Roger Federer: If that helped me?

Q. Has that positively impacted your singles play?

Roger Federer: Oh, no, no. I played two matches.

Q. But you practiced.

Roger Federer: Yeah, we practiced. I think we had two practice sessions for it. We're very professional (laughter). No, I used to play a ton of doubles when I was younger. That helped me. I don't know how many doubles tournaments I played in my life, but I played a lot, particularly my first, let's say, five years on tour. Now obviously there's just too much happening for me to play too many doubles. But I do believe, for instance, when I played more doubles in '08 Olympics, where I went and played maybe five matches, we did play some more doubles tournaments before that, I really feel that that benefited me coming into the US Open that year. I was very good at net. So I do believe that you can take away a lot from doubles because you have less time on the return and at net, as well. But this time around, no, it didn't help me unfortunately.

Q. After the match today you mentioned as you were serving for it you had some memories of the semifinal last year. Can you talk more about that.

Roger Federer: Well, I thought it was a similar atmosphere. I guess against Novak, it was later in the day. Just an assumption I have. I'm not sure anymore. I just felt the atmosphere, Labor Day weekend, also at the end, semis or finals, that those day matches have a different atmosphere to the night session matches. Now I've played two night. Coming out during the day, when I walked on, it reminded me of the ovation I got from that particular match, and then when I got up to serve for it, I think it was the same end, when it was against Novak, just tried to serve this one through. Doesn't matter whether you think about it or not. It was funny that I thought about it in a third-round match. But I'm happy that I survived it. I played a really good last game, so I'm happy.

Q. How do you feel physically after your first day match in New York's humidity? Sounds like you may have a bit of a cold. You're sniffling a bit?

Roger Federer: No, just a lot of air-conditioning in this country. I've been up and down for the last few weeks. You're right, I have a little bit of a blocked nose, but not bad. No, today honestly wasn't hot at all for me. Bit of a breeze. It almost cools you down a bit. I know when you're sitting there, it feels even warmer. For me anyway it was no problem. I enjoyed it. Had a great time out there. I was happy with my performance today.

Q. Can you compare the two quite different experiences of playing a big match on Centre Court Wimbledon versus playing on Ashe?

Roger Federer: It's great. I mean, I've played in so many places. It's true, you have to get used to some of them. Some come totally natural. Some other ones, maybe you're lacking the energy or the fire or it's almost too loud, too noisy, whatever it might be. So it takes some getting used to. Also conditions. You mentioned the heat, the humidity, the wind. Obviously indoor, outdoor tournaments have a completely different feel to them as well. People do react when it it's cold. You can't clap so much. It's cold. You have an umbrella in your hands when it's raining. Atmosphere changes. You mentioned Wimbledon and the U.S. Open. I don't want to say they could be more different, but there is a big change in it. Obviously you don't have the night sessions at Wimbledon. Now with the roof you might have some. It's not the same as here. Then you have, I don't know, advertising on change of ends. You have music, you name it, kiss cam, fan cam. It makes you laugh. The focus is obviously different. You try to find a way to handle it, and it can give you a lift when you feel the crowd is having a good time. But then also some crowds are really nice when all they care about is forehands, backhands, serves, nice tennis. There needs to be no other experience but tennis for them. Different countries, different cultures. That's what I enjoy a lot when you travel the world.

Q. You mentioned the great Dutch fans. What are the most intense fans that you played in front of?

Roger Federer: I don't know. I've had a rough one here against Andre. That was tough. And then where else? I mean, Australia, I guess, I've had a couple of tough ones, too. I've had a ton where people were cheering for me, really exciting. A lot of local home heroes throughout my career. Therefore, extra special, no doubt about it. When players have to play me back in Basel, it's also quite tricky for them.

Q. Do you feel as much pressure to win a slam now as you did before you won one?

Roger Federer: No. This is way less pressure. This is -- I don't know how to explain it. You don't even explain because it makes so much sense. Before you're trying to break through, make your move, you realize it's so hard. You still have

Agassi, Sampras, the older generation you saw from TV. Not so easy to come through that one. That's not even talking about your generation that also are pushing, trying to make their move. I remember I felt an awful lot of pressure because I was very talented and people always said, He's going to be the next No. 1, next Grand Slam champion, but it seems like there's something missing. You're like, Yeah, I agree. I agree I could maybe make it, there is something missing, but I haven't figured it out yet. So you do feel that pressure. Yeah, you panic a little bit. It's not so simple at times. Today obviously everything you have achieved, nobody can take it away from you. By virtue of that, you are much more at peace with everything that goes on in your life.

Chapter 5: On Court With 'The Maestro'...Memories of playing Federer

More ATP players discuss the special experience of playing a tennis match against Roger Federer...

Luis Horna: "The best match I ever played was against Federer in the French Open (2003). I was feeling great. Played a great match (7-6 6-2 7-6). Everything was going the way I wanted it. I played a great match and he didn't and it happened that day for me."

Rick Leach: "The first time I played him was in Monte Carlo (quarterfinal 2000). We (Leach and Ellis Ferreira) were playing Nicolas Escude and Roger on center court. And we had Prince Albert watching. And a great crowd. I knew how good he was but I wasn't really sure because I never really played him. He proceeded to almost hit a winner on every ball (Federer and Escude won 6-4 6-2). And at the time, Ellis Ferreira and I were one of the top doubles teams. We won the Australian, we got to the finals of the U.S. Open that year. Roger hit a winner on every ball. And I'm thinking to myself: 'This is the best player I've ever seen.'"

"Then I played him at the Italian Open (in 2002 with Brian MacPhie). Roger played with Tim Henman. And I booked my flight the next day because I figured we had no chance [smiles]. But that particular day I think he wasn't really thinking about doubles, he was more concerned about his singles. We actually beat them (6-3 6-1) but he didn't really have his heart into it. But I knew early on that he was something special."

"And I remember when he was coached by Peter Lundgren and I was watching him play at the U.S. Open and I'm like, If this guy could just figure out a few things, he's gonna be the best player. And it took him a little bit of time but then he got that confidence with his groundstrokes. And he always had the serve and volley and now he's got the most all-around game. To me, he's the best player ever."

Question: Do you think he did figure it all out? Or do you see any areas he can even enhance now in 2012?

Rick Leach: "Well, I think for him to consistently beat Rafa and Novak, I think he's gotta come into net a little more. And I think that's why he hired Paul Annacone, because he was such a good volleyer and doubles player. And he is starting to come in more. And the final of Wimbledon (2012) he showed he came in a lot more against Andy (Murray). He definitely has some of the best volleys in the game. But it's a shame if he doesn't come into the net."

Question: Ever talk to Roger? Any interaction with him?

Rick Leach: "I do. He's such a nice guy. He's so well-liked in the locker room. He's always saying hello to people. To me, he's just such a class guy. He'll take the time to say hello to everybody. And he doesn't have that arrogant attitude. If there's one guy that can be cocky or arrogant, it's him [smiles]."

Question: Any memorable conversations that stand out, that maybe capture his essence?

Rick Leach: "It's pretty light. I don't really want to bother him in a tournament and stuff. But he's a guy in the locker room who will talk to everybody and I personally don't really bother him in the locker room. But he will say hello to everybody and he's very well-liked in the locker room. And obviously respected."

Arnaud Clement: "What comes to mind when you think of Federer, for me, it's not a match. Federer, for me, is a gentleman on the court, in the locker room. We're very good friends. For me, he's a fantastic player and we are lucky to have had the guy as an ambassador for tennis all over the world. As an example for anybody, the kids, also for the players."

Question: Obviously it was hard to play him, what's a memory that pops out in your memory about playing him?

Clement: "Very hard to play him, of course [laughs]. I remember playing him four matches in a row - I didn't have any break points, so. And one of my weapons is my return of serve. That was funny."

1999 Marseille QF Clement 6-3 6-3
2000 Australian Open R32 Clement 6-1 6-4 6-3
2000 Halle R32 Federer 4-6 2-6

2001 Australian Open R32 Clement 7-6 6-4 6-4
2001 Davis Cup   Federer 4-6 6-3 6-7 4-6
2004 Rotterdam R32 Federer 4-6 3-6
2004 Davis Cup Federer 2-6 5-7 4-6
2004 Halle Q Federer 3-6 5-7
2006 Miami Masters R64 Federer 2-6 7-6 0-6
2010 Estoril   Q Federer 6-7 2-6
2010 Wimbledon R32 Federer 2-6 4-6 2-6

Davide Sanguinetti: "I played him three times. I lost the first two matches in Davis Cup (4-6 7-6 3-6 4-6 in 1999) and Monte Carlo (6-7 6-7 in 2001). Then we played the final of Milan in 2002. I beat him (7-6 4-6 6-1), I remember it was my first tournament win on the Tour level. And I remember I told him, 'Do not worry you will be the next No. 1 soon.' I was right. He won Wimbledon the next year."

Question: How could you tell he would be No. 1?

Davide Sanguinetti: "Just the way he was hitting the ball. For me it was easy to tell, his forehand was so heavy and his serve was so precise."

Question: Did you change your tactics for the third match with Federer in Milan after losing close matches in the first two? Or was the Italian crowd support the difference maker?

Sanguinetti: "No, I did not change my tactics. I had the crowd behind me, that gave me all the power to beat him."

Question: What were your tactics for that rematch, if you can recall?

Sanguinetti: "Open the court to his forehand and attacking on his backhand. It was really simple."

Jean-Julien Rojer: "I played him twice. We're the same age, born in 1981. I remember the first time I played against him in Rome Masters Series, he played with Yves Allegro, I played with Johan Brunstrom. And I walked on the court and I was like, 'Shit, it's Roger Federer! And how are you gonna win that one?' But it's just funny to see him, the mannerisms, just what he does, you see it on TV so many times, then you play against him. The second time we played was in Davis Cup 2012. It was a special occasion for me, we played in Holland - I play for the Netherlands now (Rojer was born in Curacao). And having a win over him there probably ranks at the top of my list. I feel like if you can beat him at anything, that's something to remember. It doesn't matter if it's backgammon [smiles]."

Question: How did you and Robin Haase pull that off?

Jean-Julien Rojer: "I'm not sure. We just played really well. Robin played really well. Roger played with Stan Wawrinka. I mean, they're really good, Olympic gold medalists, we just played really well, the crowd helped us, my family was in attendance. It was great."

Question: Did you walk on court expecting to win?

Jean-Julien Rojer: "I did actually. That match...never go on expecting to win against Roger but it was a different mindset than I had in Rome. I went on the court with a much more positive mindset and believing that we could do damage."

Question: Why were you so confident?

Jean-Julien Rojer: "I'm not sure. Just felt really good. I kept telling the guys all week that we're gonna pull out one of these matches. When we lost the two singles I told them that I still think we're gonna win one of these matches and we won the doubles."

Question: Do you have a lasting memory of Roger Federer, on court or off court?

Jean-Julien Rojer: "I think he's one of the more generous guys. When you think of him, he does so much for our sport. We're so thankful to have him. And I think it's just the kindness that he has. I mean, he's a big, big figure and he has a lot of commitments and things but he does the simple things so well - meet and greets, autographs, clinics, he does everything so graciously. And I think that's who he is. I've been around him and I know him a little bit."

Guillermo Canas: "For me, the first memory of Roger that comes to mind is when I played him and I beat him when he was really invincible. I realize this, for me, and I think for everybody, he's the most talented player that tennis has had, in all of history. And just to be a part in my life, some of this history, to beat him twice in a row in that time, it's great and I'm just so happy about that. But I think he, for me, is the most talented player, he's better than all the players we have in history."

Question: How were you able to beat him twice in a row?

Canas: "I beat him twice in a row in 2007, in Indian Wells and Miami. I don't know how. For me, it was great. I come back, I play with him first round in Indian Wells. And then I have the same chance in fourth round in Miami. And I beat him again. For me, it was great. I think one of the most important part of my career."

Question: Did you and Roger ever talk together after those matches, or about those matches?

Canas: "I'm not a friend but I have a good relationship with him. But I don't have a friendship with him. Maybe a few times we talk when we do something together but no, never, never spoke about the match. I try not (to talk tennis) with my friend or without my friend, (we talk) just about the life outside the life of the court. The tennis is just important when you go on court."

2002 Toronto Masters R64 Canas 7-6 7-5
2005 Indian Wells Masters SF Federer 3-6 1-6
2007 Indian Wells Masters R64 Canas 7-5 6-2
2007 Miami Masters R16 Canas 7-6 2-6 7-6
2007 Madrid Masters R16 Federer 0-6 3-6
2008 Rome Masters R32 Federer 3-6 3-6

Xavier Malisse: "My first match against Roger Federer was a Davis Cup (quarterfinal) match (in 1999 in Brussels). We were both dead after. I won the match in four sets (4-6 6-3 7-5 7-6). I remember I threw up after the match. It was about 102 degrees inside the arena with 4,000 people. We played for three hours 45 minutes. Just rallies, rallies, rallies. On clay, so a lot of rallies. That was tough. I couldn't do anything for three days after that match. And also the week after I got dehydrated. So that was a memorable match with Federer. The first time I played him I won. Then he won the next ten times we played."

Frank Moser: "I actually played against Federer in 1997. In the first round of qualifying in Basel. Back in the day. When I was still young and he was like a kid. It was a long match. And the umpire made a big mistake - that's what I remember. It's a really long story. You can ask him about the story, he knows [smiles]. He won (6-7 6-4) 7-5 in the third. I practiced with him in 2012 in Doha. It was a lot of fun. It's an honor for me to practice with these guys, especially Roger."

Question: Back in 1997, did you ever imagine Roger would become the player he is?

Moser: "No, not that good. But everybody said he would be like the next superstar. And I really didn't think that much about it actually. I thought he was a really good junior, he was No. 1 junior in the world at the time."

Question: Can you share a little-known fact about what it's like to play tennis with Roger?

Moser: "The ball just comes much faster than it looks, when you practice with him. You're always under pressure. And he always - wherever I hit the ball - he was already there. Like he knows where I'm hitting the ball. I don't know how he's doing it but he's doing it pretty good [smiles]."

Vince Spadea: "2006 U.S. Open third round (I played) against world No. 1 Roger Federer. I hadn't played him since 1999 in Monte Carlo when he was only 18. I closed out that match by beating Federer 6-0 in the second set, making me one of only three players to ever bagel Federer (Patrick Rafter and Byron Black also gave Fed bagels in 1999)."

"At the U.S. Open Federer started off the match a little bit shaky. At the beginning, I thought, 'This guy's not so good.' He held serve for a couple of games but I had 30-all in each return game and shanked a couple of forehands. I felt like I was playing Sampras back in the day when he'd just be coasting, still in control, but happy to make some careless mistakes. Around 3-all in the first set, Federer tightened the reigns though, and started showing the level with which he wins championships."

"He has this devastating four-shot combination. He hits a great serve, then a short-angle backhand, an inside-out forehand, and then an inside-in forehand and comes into the net. After running all over the court to retrieve his shots, I invariably would pop a ball up and he would knock it off with an easy volley winner."

"Federer's got a lot of different shot varieties, a lot of different paces and depths he hits to. He almost never hits the ball to the same spot on the court during a rally. He hits every part of the inside of the court. There's not a real pattern of where he's going to hit the ball. Sometimes on his inside-out forehand, he angles it inside the box with heavy spin. Sometimes he loops a blooper. And sometimes he hits it more left of center."

"His backhand he'll hit with heavy topspin or angle it wide cross-court. His backhand down the line is nicely disguised so that he hits it early or even late. He hits this shot at critical moments and gains a big advantage in the rally against anyone."

"Most impressive was his aggressive serving under pressure at deuce or break points. His placement on his serve and his fearlessness to unleash big shots, to paint lines under pressure, is his greatest talent. Anyone who can play 15-40 the same way he plays 40-love, going for all his shots and making most of them, possesses a special gift. Some people may call it confidence. I call it 'Federence.'"

It's unparalleled shot-making combined with confidence."

"He plays a 5-all game in the fifth set like he's up 6-0, 5-0. That's how championships are won. The human reaction is always to tighten up, retreat, and hope something good happens. But instead, Federer says to himself, 'Something's going to happen. And I'm going to be the one who does it - something aggressive and toxic to my opponent."

"After losing the first two sets 6-3, 6-3, against Federer, I felt like I wasn't doing enough, when actually I was doing everything I could do. I was just being outplayed. But instead of continuing to play the same way, I decided to employ the Rod Laver tactic of 'Never change a winning game, always change a losing game.' I changed a losing game, but unfortunately for a bigger losing game, and I lost the last set 6-0. They say you've got to take big risks to net big gains (unless you're playing Roger Federer). So I went for the gusto and got the busto."

"I like Federer. He's very friendly and out-of-the-ordinary nice. The other day I was in the U.S. Open locker room and I was looking up at a television and a voice rang out behind me, 'Hey Vince. How are you?' I looked around and it was Federer. I thought, 'I haven't spoken to this guy in a little while. We've had minimal conversations. But still he makes an effort to get to know me and most everyone else on Tour. I think that's what keeps him humble, but still hungry."

[Spadea's comments are from his acclaimed book "Break Point: The Secret Diary Of A Pro Tennis Player.]

Lleyton Hewitt: "He's so good at dictating play, playing on his terms. It's very hard on his service games to try - you're sort of trying to hang into his service games. You can't really play the style of tennis that you want to play out there. That's the hard thing. When he is able to play the way he wants to play and dictate terms, he's going to be very tough to beat. Obviously, he's got a lot of pressure on him and every time he steps out here at the moment purely because he's won so many big matches out there and everyone expects him to keep winning. Yeah, in terms of that, obviously, how capable, how good he can play if he's on, but you've got to try and take those small opportunities when they come. You're going to get some out there but you're not going to get a lot, obviously."

"He wants to dictate play so much, and he doesn't give you the opportunity to try and do different things against him too much. In his service games he plays at his pace and yeah, he's got a great serve. It's not the biggest serve out there but he hits his spots and he hits them extremely well to set up his next shot. That's what he does so different to a guy like Roddick, who is going to hit through you a lot more on the serve. Whereas Roger sets up his serve, obviously for his strengths."

Question: You've played a lot of the tennis greats in your career, where do you rate Roger with the other top players you've competed against?

Hewitt: "Oh, he's as good as there is, there's no doubt, that I've played. He's got the most all-around game, I think, that I've ever played. Obviously, Agassi and Sampras were both greats, and I was able to play both of them when they were still at their best, winning Grand Slams, both of them. Roger has been able to take the game to a new level and I think the most complete player for sure is Roger."

Jeff Coetzee: "I have played Rog a couple times in doubles. I was lucky enough at the 2007 Shanghai Masters Cup to have warmed him up for his semi final match (before Federer defeated Nadal 64 61). His first couple balls he hit with two hands (imitating Coetzee who hits double-handed forehands and backhands). We always chatted when he has a moment and he always asked about South Africa. Roger Federer is the most humble guy I have known."

Question: What do you remember about the matches against Roger?

Coetzee: "The matches were always close and like a true champ Rog lifted his game. The first time we played was at Wimbledon (2001 R64), he and Wayne Ferreira beat me and Brent Haygarth in four sets (7-6 5-7 4-6 5-7). The second time was in Vienna (QF 2003). Federer and Yves Allegro beat me and Chris Haggard (3-6 4-6)."

Bernard Tomic interview after losing to Federer 6-4 7-6 6-1 at 2013 Australian Open third round:

"A lot of players, especially in the locker room, they idolize Roger. You want to pick up anything you can from this sort of a player. He is the greatest our sport's ever had. You learn something every time you watch him. I learned something tonight as well."

"You use this and you use it in a good way. It's going to make me a better player. I'm going to keep working hard. Point by point, I'm going to get my opportunities this year again and become a better player."

Q. The choice of serving first, did you get the choice?

Bernard Tomic: "Yeah. I elected to serve considering I was serving really well the last few weeks. But that didn't matter first service game (smiling)."

Q. Not a great start. Were there a few nerves, a bit tight?

Bernard Tomic: "Yeah, with sort of him, he starts really well. That sort of player starts really well. He always puts his opponent down."

"A lot of players, when you play these sort of players like Roger or Novak, you lose belief before you get into the match. 80 or 90% of players that play the top guys, like with Roger, you lose your belief."

"I got in there (on court), I started to think after they mentioned all these Grand Slams leading up, Wimbledon champion six times, six times U.S. Open champion (laughter). Then I was, Oh, crap, it's Roger. I try to block out who's on the other side of the net but couldn't quite do it after that announcement."

"Yeah, but then that first service game was important. I lost it. Then I was like, Oh, no."

Q. How different was your mindset going in to face Roger tonight compared with last year?

Bernard Tomic: "A lot different. You know, I was confident that I could have pushed it. I had a lot more chances than I did last year. I played a lot better than I did last year."

"Anything could have happened if I had won that important point in the tiebreak. Giving myself two or three set points would you have been huge to turn the match around."

"When he needs it the most, he plays amazing. Today I didn't hit the right shot, didn't play the right point when I needed to. He played the right tennis."

Q. Did he say anything in particular to you after the game at the net?

Bernard Tomic: "Yeah. He said, 'Keep going, you improved.' Every time I played him, he mentioned, 'Well done, Bernie, keep going, keep improving,' which is a good thing, hearing that from somebody that's giving some advice. Keep going, keep pushing yourself."

"It's important you take that onboard because, you know, you can become a better player when you get information off the world's best. You take that onboard and then you can use that to work on whatever you need to work on."

"Right now I need to improve. I'm going to keep improving. I've improved a lot. But to become someone like him, or even in that area, I've got to improve more."

Q. Compare this to the previous meeting.

Bernard Tomic: "Yeah. Just showed me that I'm playing better each year. You know, I'm pushing myself in the off season. That's why I'm playing the tennis I'm playing."

"He beat me. I'm satisfied with the result here in Melbourne, especially the last few weeks. Just need to see what he does this tournament. I'm backing him to win. I'm sure he has a good chance of winning."

"And, yeah, it's always a good feeling if you can lose to the champion (smiling)."

David Nalbandian speaking about his success against Federer at Masters Cup in 2003:

"I think every match is different, it's completely different. I think when you go out in the court, it's something special you feel inside. But you never know. With this kind of players, every time you go out the court, it's completely different. Very hard, very tough match. So every time I play with Roger was very tough match - always three sets or four sets in the U.S. Open. So he's a very good player. But I like (playing) against him. I feel comfortable when I play against him. I know him, I don't know, five years ago when we were juniors. So we have a lot of matches and many years practicing and playing matches. So I know him a little more than other ones."

"Against him, you need to play very good from everywhere. I think that I do it."

"I said before, every time we play, the match is very close, is very tough. So I don't know what's gonna happen next match. I hope don't play this long, but is gonna be a tough either way. Doesn't matter who's leading in the history."

On beating Federer in the final of 2005 Masters Cup in Shanghai from two sets down after losing four previous matches to Federer:

David Nalbandian: "It's incredible when you are two sets to down, it's really difficult to come back. Today, of course it's much different, much, much important. Against Roger, you can't play bad if you want to win. Again, losing two sets to love and come back against him, incredible."

At Australian Open 2006:

David Nalbandian: "I play against him a lot of time from juniors. I mean, we're talking about maybe almost ten years ago or nine years ago, so we know each other very good. We know each other that every time we go out on the court, it's going to be a very good match, a very fight match. It's good. I always enjoy to playing against him. I'm happy to be in the history beating him, so it's okay."

Question at 2006 Masters Series Miami

Q. As a player who has a good record against him, what do you think is the secret of beating Federer?

David Nalbandian: "I like to play against him. I don't know exactly the secret, but I like really enjoy it every time we play each other."

Pete Sampras Interview after losing to Federer at Wimbledon 2001:

Q. What emotions are playing out in your head now?

Pete Sampras: "Well, just very -- I'm very disappointed obviously. I lost to a really, really good player today. He played great. He's a great shot-maker. He won the big points. I had my chances throughout the match, had a couple breakpoints there in the fifth. You know, he came up with some really good stuff at huge times. He played a great game to break me. I give him a lot of credit. He really played very well."

Q. As Centre Court debuts go, have you ever seen anyone quite so composed as that?

Pete Sampras: "Yeah, he was very relaxed. His demeanor on the court is pretty similar to mine. He's pretty relaxed. Goes out and plays. Doesn't get too emotional, too many highs and lows. He's got a great backhand, serves well. He's definitely got a good all-around court game. Doesn't have any holes in his game. Great athlete. I mean, he really played really well. You know, just getting off the court, I'm disappointed, I mean, obviously. You know, I had a few chances. I felt like I had it at 4-all. Hit a good return. You know, wasn't to be. You know, I came up a little bit short."

Q. When was the last time you felt so near defeat here at Wimbledon?

Pete Sampras: "Well, four years ago."

Q. When you lost, when you felt so near, when you felt so much in danger of losing.

Pete Sampras: "Well, there's always a threat of losing out there when it's close. You know, I've won my fair share of close matches out there over the years. And today, just came up a little bit short. You know, majority of the time I've gotten my breaks, I've gotten that crucial shot at crucial points in the match. Today, you know, I had a chance there, and I didn't convert. I give him a lot of the credit, you know, the way he played."

Q. You've had so many great moments on that court. What were the emotions as you were walking off?

Pete Sampras: "Well, it was his moment. I mean, he really played a great match. His first match out there. You know, I give him a lot of credit for handling it very well. It's grass court tennis, it goes by pretty quick. One minute you feel like you have it, and the next minute you're walking off the court. Just disappointed. It's rare that I've lost, you know, a close match here at Wimbledon. But, you know, you know something so great isn't going to last forever. Today I just came up a little bit short."

Q. There are other Roger Federers out there, as you well know. Jim Courier says they're coming out of the woodwork, young players with a lot of talent. For you, do you now redouble your efforts, work even harder, or do you sit down sometime after the emotions have passed and start considering what you want to do in the future?

Pete Sampras: "Well, sure, there are a lot of young guys coming up, and Roger is one of them. But I think he's a little extra special than some of the other guys. I mean, he's got a really good all-around court game. You know, all I can try to do is rebound from kind of a disappointing year and get ready for the summer. It's going to take me a while to get over this one. But just keep trying to work hard, do the training, put in the practise hours on the court, and hopefully I can have a good summer. Maybe The Open can be a little bit better than here. It's disappointing. It's a tough, tough loss, you know, to deal with."

Q. Can you size up your run here at Wimbledon, now that it's over for the time being?

Pete Sampras: "Well, it's the run, like I said, it wasn't going to last forever. You know, I've won a lot of close matches out there - last year's final. Over the years, you know, I've gotten a little bit fortunate. Today I didn't get it. You know, I really felt, you know, I was very much in contention out there, very much felt like I was going to win. But, you know, to have been so dominant over the years, it obviously gets more difficult as the years go on to keep on staying dominant. Today was an occasion of, you know, played really well at the right time. That's the key to grass. He picked it up when he had to. He played a great match."

Q. Do you think this result will make you think more about not playing here in the near future, that you may not be back a year or two years from now?

Pete Sampras: "Well, let's not get carried away. I mean, I just lost. I plan on being back for many years. I mean, this is why I play, for these tournaments. You know, I feel the reason I'd stop, it won't be because of my ability; it will be because I don't want to do it anymore. There's no reason to, you know, panic and think that I can't come back here and win here again. I feel like I can always win here."

Q. Was there any sense even from the start of the Championships that perhaps something inside you said, "It might not be this year"? You had tough matches all the way through, surprisingly tough from what we've seen of you in the past. Was there something nagging in the back of your mind?

Pete Sampras: "Well, there's always a fear of that, like my run's going to end. Those are thoughts that come in and out of your head. But when you go out and compete, you compete, and you don't thhink about negative thoughts. But, you know, like I said, nothing is so great, like this tournament has been over the years to me, is going to last forever. Occasionally you're going to lose a tough match, and it happened today. You know, I lost to Roger, who was playing great at the time. I thought I played pretty well. You know, I felt like I had some chances. But it's unfortunate it's over."

Q. A decade ago you had a match against Lendl at Flushing Meadows that you had your breakthrough on, similar round I think, too. Did this match have that kind of feel, but you were on the other end of it?

Pete Sampras: "I mean, not really. That match -- no. I mean, I really haven't thought about that. You know, I lost to a talented player that's a great shot-maker, similar to the way I was when I was younger, and still today. He's got a great grass court game. He's got all the tools."

Q. You hit with Roger before. When he beat the Americans in the Davis Cup, did you ask Todd Martin or Jan-Michael Gambill about him at all?

Pete Sampras: "I've seen Roger play. I've practiced with him. I had a pretty good idea of what he wanted to do out there. You know, he's got a good all-around court game. Doesn't have any holes. It's a little different when you compete against him. His serve, I couldn't really get ahold of. His shots, he was on. You know, I've seen him play enough over the years to kind of know what to expect."

Q. Take us back to that ninth game of that fifth set when you had some break opportunities. What was he doing to prevent you from getting through, where normally you would get through in that situation?

Pete Sampras: "Well, on one of them, one of my best forehand returns, got it down to his feet. He kind of picked it up and had a backhand there that I didn't hit all that well. The other one, I kind of hit it, a conservative chip to his forehand. He hit a good forehand winner. You know, I give him credit, he came up with some good stuff when he had to, won the big point. I could possibly break him there, I think I could go on to win this match. But it wasn't to be."

Attila Savolt discusses 2002 Australian Open match vs. Federer
(R64 2-6 5-7 4-6)

Question: What is your first memory of Roger Federer?

Attila Savolt: "That's a tough question. I don't really remember anything before the match we played in 2002. I already knew about him, that he was really an up and coming star, everybody was talking about him. In 2001, that was my first year in the top 100, so before I was more on the Challenger tour. In 2001 and 2002 I started to see him around in the locker room. A lot of people were talking about him already, as a very good talent. But the first experience - I didn't have a chance to practice with him - the first experience was the match at the Australian Open."

Question: Any memory of him before the match in the locker room? Jan-Michael Gambill told me Marcelo Rios tried to stare him down before they played.

Attila Savolt: "No, it was absolutely nothing like that. It was a night match, there was nobody anymore in the locker room. We were the last match of the day. It was basically just both of us - he was in one corner with his coach who was Peter Lundgren at the time, and I was with my coach in the other corner. We didn't exchange anything before the match. He was young. I think he was 19 then, and I have to say, I really had the impression that he was kind of cocky, especially with Peter, together. Not only at Australian Open but then after I saw him in Miami, then we practiced, I got to know him a little better, not too close though. He really was a young, upcoming guy. He was already getting the attention, he was already top 10, future star. And with Lundgren, they were kind of walking around. I remember my girlfriend that time, who's my wife now, she was always telling me how much this guy (Federer) is staring at me, many times. Although that time, I think Federer, he was already with Mirka. I think they came together at the Olympics in 2000. So he must have been in a relationship. But you know, looking at girls is okay, right [smiles]?"

Question: He's a normal guy [smile]. So the match starts on Stadium court.

Attila Savolt: "We got on pretty late. And I really thought that I had good chance. He was 9 or 10 or 11 in the world. I definitely never had strong in my mind that he was going to be as good as he became. I think nobody really did. Everybody was talking of him as a future star, very, very good potential. But I never really heard anybody saying that he could be the best ever. And I certainly didn't feel that way on the court."

"Although I think I played a bad match there. I wasn't in good shape at all. I won my first round, struggling in five sets (vs. Olivier Patience 6-3 3-6 6-3 3-6 6-4). And I was very, very disappointed after the match. The whole match. I really felt there was so much more in the match for me. I lost in three sets. I was a break up in the second set, two breaks up in the third set. I had a lot of chances to make it close. I'm not saying to win, but to make it closer. But, for sure, I never forget the second set. Set point that I had on him. It was 5-4 for me, he was serving, 30-40. And he just played one of those unbelievable points that he's played like a thousand times...the really important point."

"I really felt I hit an unbelievable pass. I already saw the ball passed him. And he just hit two unbelievable reflex volleys. I never forget that. Set point. That really stayed with me. Because if I won the second set, you never really know what comes after that. So he really showed there - not really with anything else - after the match I was really more angry at myself after the match because I really felt I had a lot of chances. But at that point he showed some little bit of this extra that made him such a good player after that."

Question: What were you trying to do against him? What was your strategy? Were you able to find any holes or weaknesses in his game?

Attila Savolt: "Yes. I definitely had a clear, clear tactic with my coach which was attacking on his backhand. I wasn't particularly really an aggressive player going to the net but in that match I was definitely trying to and looking to get to the net on his backhand. His backhand was definitely the weakpoint of his game, a little bit, stayed with him throughout his whole career, a little bit. So I was trying to serve and volley to his backhand. Chip a lot to his backhand. Trying to go to the net on his backhand. And that was definitely the tactic."

Question: What did he try to do against you?

Attila Savolt: "He played from the baseline. He played pretty similar as he's playing now. He didn't come too much to the net. He was serving well. He was definitely placing his serves well. He played very similar as he does now. He really had everything there. Just a little, small mistakes. For me, a little bit less power. He was very fluent and very relaxed in the whole match."

Question: You had no idea he would become the No. 1 player, all-time great player, from that match?

Attila Savolt: "No. No. I didn't see that at all. I'm not saying - he was already top 10 at 19 - obviously you have a good chance to be No. 1. I'm not saying that I didn't feel he was going to be a Grand Slam champion or he was going to be a really good player. But I never thought he was going to be best there ever was."

Question: Is there any other player you played in your career that, after you played them, you thought, 'Wow, this guy is really good.' You were really impressed by them. And you thought they had the talent to become something special?

Attila Savolt: "I had one match against (David) Nalbandian, that I left the court and I thought: 'What happened on the court here?' Because it was like so quickly over (2-6, 1-6 R16 Sopot, Poland outdoor red clay in 2001). And I didn't really feel...I felt like every ball was coming back. And every ball he was placing very good. I had a feeling that he would do much better than he ended up. He was very good."

"Then I remember I had a practice with (Rafael) Nadal when he was 15. He was unbelievable. He was hitting the ball so hard that day. Just at a practice. That was maybe 2002 or 2003 at a Challenger in France, like $150,000 Challenger. And we just hit the balls for an hour. And he was hitting unbelievable. And he had such an intensity and everything already at the age of 15. He was like a full player. Normally at the age of 15, you're playing the junior tournaments, you're acting kind of like a junior and everything. He was already so professional. He already knew what he was doing so much. And he was so dedicated."

Question: You also played Marcelo Rios (6-1, 6-2 loss in Palermo on outdoor clay in 2002). How was the experience of playing Rios compare to playing Federer?

Attila Savolt: "Very different styles. With Federer, I felt all the match (his) intensity. With Rios, I really felt he was more like playing on the court. He was playing on the court. I definitely felt against Rios that I didn't have the weapon or I didn't find the way to put him in trouble or how to beat him. Against Federer, at the end of the match I had the feeling I could have done so much more, if I play better. Against Rios, I didn't feel good on the court. I felt that the way he played, it was very uncomfortable for me. Like, the angles that he was playing, the rhythm that he changed. I didn't like the game, he was very effective."

Question: After your match with Federer, you practiced with him later and got to know him a bit better?

Attila Savolt: "I don't remember the year. I remember we practiced together one practice session at the French Open. Probably the next year. Then the same year at Indian Wells we had a practice but we never really developed any close relations."

Question: Was he friendly or more business-like at practice?

Attila Savolt: "He was very friendly at practice. With Lundgren, they would always be laughing, relaxed, always in a very good mood. It was a nice energy around them, even on the practice court. They don't take it so serious. They were joking around, they were very relaxed, really enjoying time together. I really thought that they really fit together very well."

Question: I have seen Federer practice at majors, he often sits together with the other player like Mardy Fish or Stefan Koubek on breaks, chatting away. Very few players do that at majors, they stay apart, with their teams. Federer is unique in that way.

Attila Savolt: "I think also Lundgren was an effect on him. He's a very open guy, very relaxed, very nice guy too. I found that they really fit together. There was always a smile on both of their faces."

Question: Federer gets along with everybody too, is there any player that does not like him, that you can think of?

Attila Savolt: "No. Because he's really open, not too much, you know, unless, I guess, he has a couple of good, close friends. But he was really open to everybody. Not very close but always nice, always open. Very polite, always. That's what makes him such a big champion and everybody likes this. You can hardly find anything in his career that anybody can say anything bad about him.

That, in my eyes, the bigger champion you are, the bigger personality you are. That's what I believe. Nadal was the same. (Andre) Agassi, for me, was the same."

Question: Lasting memory of Roger?

Attila Savolt: "Well, that was a memory that was not face to face with him. But I had the Swiss management when I was playing. And they owned the Gstaad tournament. And then when I stopped playing in 2004, it was probably around 2005 and I wanted to get in touch with him. Because I wanted to write a book in Hungarian. And I wanted to ask him to write a couple of quotes in the beginning, like a foreword. And so I tried to get in touch through my ex-agent who was his. They were pretty close. And in a couple of weeks I got a response through the agent from Federer, that he was very happy, thank you very much for asking, he remembers me very much, I played very well, he said that I stopped too early, and sorry that he had to say no because he had so many requests like this. It was a very polite no. So that was my last memory of him actually."

Bjorn Phau discusses 1999 Washington, DC victory vs. Roger Federer...

"Our match was in 1999. He was, like, coming up, he was ranked like 90. And it was in Washington. He was in main draw, I qualified. And I played him first round. I beat him easy. I think he didn't get along with the heat. He was really struggling with the heat. And he wasn't the Roger Federer he got to be. But, of course, I have a win on my record against Roger Federer [smiles]."

Question: Did you ever talk about that match since with him?

Bjorn Phau: "Actually not. But I think he knows."

Question: Practice with him?

Bjorn Phau: "A couple of times."

Question: Lasting memory for you of Roger Federer?

Bjorn Phau: "Being really polite. Always saying hi. There are also some players who don't see you. So he's really polite and a nice guy."

1999 Washington R64   Phau   6-2, 6-3
2007 Australian Open R128   Federer   5-7, 0-6, 4-6
2010 Estoril R16   Federer 3-6, 4-6
2012 U.S. Open R 64   Federer   2-6, 3-6, 2-6

Andre Sa: "I played him 2004 Australian Open. It was great to play him at that time. He was becoming very famous. He won the tournament that year and became No. 1, so people were talking about him all the time. It was just great to be able to play on the court against him. And, at the time, not the greatest but one of the best players that I have ever seen hitting the ball. It was just a great, fun experience. I played with my friend Flavio Saretta, also from Brazil, which was nice, so we had a pretty good crowd. Federer was playing with Yves Allegro, his fellow countryman from Davis Cup."

Question: Who won?

Andre Sa: "We ended up winning 6-4 6-4, which was a really good run for us."

Question: Your first memory of Federer?

Andre Sa: "Well, I think when I was starting to play professional in 1998, I saw this kid, he won junior Wimbledon. That was the first time I've ever seen him play. And I knew everybody was really talking about this kid, he won the title there, playing so smooth and graceful that everybody knew he was gonna be good."

Question: You saw him play juniors at Wimbledon?

Andre Sa: "I saw him play."

Question: You knew he would be good?

Andre Sa: "I knew it, man."

Question: Have you shared many conversations with Federer over the years?

Andre Sa: "Yeah, many times conversations. The last couple years I'm a member of the ATP Player Council. He's the president. So we talk a lot and discuss the issues on tennis and the game. And it's unbelievable how committed he is. I mean, he's giving so much time to take care of the player's problems. It's just great."

Question: Lasting memory of Federer?

Andre Sa: "The memory I have most recently is on the Council. To give that much time to other people's problems just shows a lot of character. He has a lot of influence on the decisions that are made on the Council. So for him to be there five, six hours, sitting through meetings discussing other player's problems is just something that I find unbelievable."

Mischa Zverev quotes after losing to Federer 0-6 0-6 in the quarterfinal at 2013 Halle tournament: "With Federer, it's like you're at the net and you think, 'Oh why did I even come here?' Because his preparation for the shot is unbelievable. My coach said that with him, he's always on the ground, he's always stable, he's never off balance and you cannot tell where the hell he's going to hit the ball. So it was a disadvantage to come to the net today."

"His ball when it travels to the air, it has so much stuff on it, like it just only goes through the air but it moves like left and right, it moves like a shank but it's not a shank. You think it's going to go long but it's like two feet inside the baseline. His ball is just phenomenal. The worst is like when you're at the net you cannot tell where he's going to go. With most of the players, you can anticipate. Because of his (stance), he can go down the line or crosscourt. You think, 'Okay he went down the line most of the times, so let's cover down the line.'"

"I'm a huge fan of Federer, I watch pretty much every match of his. When he loses, I never have a feeling he loses matches because he's not good enough, it's mainly because he's either a little bit injured or it's like a mental thing with him. So, I'm not saying he's mentally weak [smiles]. I'm just saying he's a phenomenal player, he still is. He still has the game to beat anyone like easily."

Cyril Saulnier: "I remember I played him two times. It was many years ago. It was really nice to play against him. Just a good feeling to play him. The first time it was in Marseille (R32 6-7 4-6 in 2001). He was ranked around 60. It was his second year after the juniors. He was really talented, for sure. Great player. We played a great match. I lost but I think he was like he is today, a top top player. And then the second time it was in Milan, Italy (R16 6-2 3-6 4-6 in 2001). I lost but he was starting to play much, much better, his ranking was somewhere around 20."

Question: Super impressed by his game? Did you think he would become what he became?

Cyril Saulnier: "No, no, no. I think no. Okay, he was talented, he had many shots on his racquet but we cannot predict what he would become, No. 1 and the best player in the world for many years. I was not expecting this. But with hard work and many things, you can reach what he did. So that's pretty amazing."

Question: Off court memory of Federer?

Cyril Saulnier: "He is a really nice guy. Very humble. Always joking. And we can discuss about everything. Most always the same. I met him again in Roland Garros 2009. He was always the same. I think it's very important to be a champion in the court and off the court."

Question: Lasting memory of Federer?

Cyril Saulnier: "I worked after my career at the French Open and I was a sports coordinator. And I was like a player liasion. And I was in charge about the relation with the players, women and men. And in the year 2009 when he won Roland Garros it was a great memory. He won the tournament so it was pretty amazing."

Tom Vanhoudt: "I played him in Miami in doubles, quarters. I remember he was experimenting with his serve. He was hitting first serves that were very slow and then go for the second. I've never seen anybody mix up their serves that much. At the time I think he was No. 30. He was mixing the pace and a lot of kick. He was keeping you guessing."

Jesse Levine practiced with Federer in Dubai in July 2007.

"Anytime you can play with the best in the game in any sport it's a pretty amazing experience. So, for me, I've been able to do it a couple of times now. And it was an amazing experience and anytime he calls back to do it again I'm definitely up for it."

Question: What do you feel you gained from this experience?

Jesse Levine: "Just some tips here and there that he would help me out with. Some shots that he felt that I could improve on. Some shots that I could have done a little bit better. Or that he thought that I did well. It was a good experience, he kind of gave a good grasp of things and he's a pretty knowledgable guy and a really classy guy on and off the court."

Question: How do you feel you performed while practicing and working with him?

Jesse Levine: "It was great. It was a long time ago. A really long time ago [smiles]. It was while I was in college. So I still see him all the time now and we get along really well."

Question: Can you share a lasting memory of Roger, on or off court, maybe a conversation, anything?

Jesse Levine: "He's really into hockey. We like to mess around with hockey because I'm a big Ottawa Senators fan, he always give me crap because they barely made the playoffs this year [smiles]."

Question: Who is he a fan of?

Jesse Levine: "He likes Swiss League teams. He doesn't really follow the NHL but he likes (Alexander) Ovechkin and (Sidney) Crosby."

Cedrik-Marcel Stebe practiced with Roger Federer in Dubai in February 2012.

Question: How did you arrange to practice with Roger Federer?

Cedrik-Marcel Stebe: "Actually, he watched my match last year in the Australian Open against Lleyton Hewitt on television. And I met him actually in the locker room. We just started talking and he said maybe we can practice sometime. And then in Dubai I went down a few days early and we just had a good hit."

Question: Describe the feeling to be on the court with Roger Federer?

Cedrik-Marcel Stebe: "Actually, first time I was a bit nervous. It was a bit hard for me because I had just come from the indoor season. I was just practicing indoors. And the first time I practiced outdoors I was really nervous. I wasn't hitting my best tennis. I just felt like I cannot play tennis. I don't like the way I hit with him."

Question: When was this?

Cedrik-Marcel Stebe: "February 2012."

Question: Why is he so difficult to play?

Cedrik-Marcel Stebe: "Well, actually any shot you make, hit the line or something if you think you make a good shot, he's just there and puts it back and plays even a better shot. It's a strange feeling with everything coming back. And everything you do is just being outplayed."

Question: Did you get more comfortable and confident as the week went on?

Cedrik-Marcel Stebe: "Yeah, actually at the end we just played a few sets as well. At first I wasn't able to break him at all. And by the end I was playing better and better. He had a hard time playing against me as well."

Question: Why do you think that was?

Cedrik-Marcel Stebe: "Well, I started to relax more. He was just being a nice guy anyway. He was talking to me a lot, just giving me a few tips. He's a really nice guy."

Question: Did the experience help you?

Cedrik-Marcel Stebe: "It was really nice. I found my game a little bit better afterwards. When I played Djokovic in the first round there (in Dubai), it was tough to play him. I had my chances there as well. So I felt it helped me a lot to practice with him. He showed me just how much I have to work on. But I think it's good."

Question: Keep in touch with Roger?

Cedrik-Marcel Stebe: "At Grand Slams I always talk with him. We talk about doing another practice session together but right now my ranking is not that good. So we just have to wait till I'm back to top 100 or better."

Question: Lasting memory or image of Roger, on or off court?

Cedrik-Marcel Stebe: "Actually, he's a really nice guy. He's really relaxed on court. He just loves the game. Just loves playing tennis, for all his life already. A perfect tennis player. Perfect guy."

(Note: After this interview, Stebe played Federer in the R16 at 2013 Halle and lost 3-6 3-6.)

Roman Borvanov practiced with Federer in Indian Wells.

Question: How did you get the chance to practice with Roger Federer in Indian Wells?

Roman Borvanov: "I put my name down looking for practice at the tournament desk. And the person who was in charge told me, 'Hey Roman, someone is looking to practice.' And I said, 'I think I'm already set.' He's like, 'Too bad, because Federer is looking to hit.' I was like: 'Oh, really? I think I might change my plans [smiles].' So obviously it would be on the center court in Indian Wells, which is the second-largest arena in the U.S. I said, 'Sure, let's go practice with Federer.'"

"And so I get there and I meet Federer, which is really cool. He was there with his fitness trainer. He just arrived from Europe. It was his first day of practice, so I knew we were not gonna play points, we'll just do a lot of practicing. And then we meet. And he actually said he needed about 30 minutes to do some warm-up. So I said, 'Okay.' And I started watching what he's doing. And he went with his fitness coach and did this whole routine of warming up his legs. He did a lot of fast feet exercises like mini soccer and doing figure eight with his little soccer ball around these tennis balls. So, like a lot of coordination exercises. He did some core and jump rope. So he was doing a series of exercises for 30 minutes. Then he said, 'Okay, I'm ready, we can go.'"

"So he did a lot of activation even before we went to practice. Then we started hitting. For me It was very Interesting just to see how he hit balls. To feel his ball was a very unique experience because the ball was rotating in so many different ways. He is able to hit balls like no other. I practiced with many guys on the Tour, it was incredible. He could spin the ball like topspin, sideways, underspin, so many different ways he could hit the ball, I thought it was unbelievable. Now I realize how he's able to hit the forehand inside out and it tails away. Not many guys can hit the ball like that or have such a good sensation of the ball. He asked me to move him around a little bit. So I think that practice was more for him than for me, which I didn't mind. We just hit some serves and returns. He told me we might practice again and play points but he canceled on me the next day [smiles]."

"So I didn't get a chance to play some points with him but it was a good experience. Especially on center court where it's different, it's not like on outside courts. The wind bounces off the stadium in so many different directions. When you hit the ball in the court level, you think the wind is blowing this way but then the ball would completely change with speed because 20 or 30 feet higher, the direction of the wind is completely different. So I think practice on the center court is an advantage, especially if you know you're gonna play there, and he always does, so. That was my experience."

Question: Any conversation?

Roman Borvanov: "Yes, I had a little conversation. He asked me about my rank, about what type of tournaments I'm playing and where I'm going. Then I asked him how his family is doing and we had one mutual friend. I started out on the Tour with one Swiss guy who also went to college in Oregon, I asked about him. They grew up in juniors, the same age. He just said he was lucky that he never had to go through playing on the Futures tour, he's glad he was kind of lucky that he was able to skip that, get some wildcards and be on his way to the top 100, which I don't blame him."

Question: Lasting memory or impression of Roger, on or off court?

Roman Borvanov: "That he was a very genuine guy. I was a little nervous at first. He was very cool, very relaxed. I understand it was his first hit, he wasn't gearing up for his match."

Question: Ever see him since?

Roman Borvanov: "Actually, no. Federer only plays Grand Slams and I was only able to go to a few Grand Slams but I always play the qualies so I don't usually cross paths. I'm pretty sure he would remember me."

Steve Johnson: "I practiced with him a few times, probably about a dozen times. And he's one of the nicest guys ever. Eventhough he's one of the best players of all time, he still remembers everybody he hits with and some of the little guys. So it's very special for us."

Question: Can you describe the feeling of what it's like to be on the court with Roger?

Steve Johnson: "It's nerve-wracking [smiles]. I mean, it's nerve-wracking at the beginning, you don't want to be the guy that he doesn't ask again, something like that. You're just nervous. You want to make as many balls as possible. But he's a great guy. He makes you feel comfortable. He's pretty down to earth and just a funny guy. He's really, I think, one of the nicest guys on the Tour."

Question: When was the first time you hit with him?

Steve Johnson: "Cincinnati in 2011."

Question: Eleven times since?

Steve Johnson: "Yeah, we practiced three times there. A couple of times at the U.S. Open. This past Indian Wells. You can learn a lot from him. It's nice for us. I feel like I can go ask him anything and he'll give me a straight answer. You feel like he's always there to help you if you needed it."

Mark Knowles: "I've known Federer for a long time, probably since he first came on Tour. He's probably the classiest champion that we've ever had. Obviously his results and his play speaks for itself. But it's really who he is off the court that's even better than that. He's as good as advertised, great guy, and I think that reflects on the fact that all of his peers speak so highly of him. Usually if you have somebody that dominates a sport so much, there's bound to be a few bad things said at some point from your peers. He's as advertised. He's one of the greatest players that we've ever seen. Definitely the most talented guy that we've seen. And such a cool demeanor. Really represents us, not only on the court as I mentioned, but a guy who's been president of the ATP Council for a number of years. He's active in meetings, all the meanwhile balancing a family with a lovely wife and two twin daughters. So he's a complete package, if you look up 'complete package' in the dictionairy it's Roger Federer."

Question: Lasting memory of Roger Federer, on or off court, which captures his essence?

Mark Knowles: "I think how relaxed he is. It's hard to imagine how relaxed he really is. I've played him a lot and it can be disconcerting how relaxed he is when you look across at the other side of the net and realize he handles tension a little bit differently than others. He does a great job of channeling it and not wearing it on his sleeve, per se. And he's the same off the court. He always looks like he's cool, calm and in control. And he doesn't seem to get flustered very often. A cool, classy guy."

Question: Is there anything you dislike about him?

Mark Knowles: "Yeah, usually you can find something to dislike about somebody. And you can dig really hard. Honestly, there's nothing I dislike about him. Except that he's a way better tennis player than I ever was [smiles]. But that's more of a credit to him. He's really mastered the game and so, unfortunately, there's not a bad thing I can say about him."

Chapter 6: Federer & Nadal

In 2008 just before the U.S. Open, Federer and Nadal participated in a unique Nike press conference titled "Grapple In The Apple" with boxing promoter Don King at the Mandarin Hotel on W. 60th Street. Both Nadal and Federer faced questions asked by New York City school kids and each answered as follows...

Question: What inspired you to try a pro career in tennis?

Nadal: "When I was 10-12 years old I started playing well and maybe at that moment I started thinking I can be a pro. You never know how hard it is to be a professional player. So just I try my best and finally I did it."

Federer: "Watching my idols play back at Wimbledon or at the U.S. Open, wanting to be maybe like them one day. Practice hard. Maybe when I was #1 junior I was 17 years old. I hoped to maybe one day maybe equal that feat on the mens tour, also become #1 in the world there. So I'm happy I chose tennis, put it that way."

Question: What was the highlight of your Olympics experience in Beijing?

Federer: "Well, for me it's been my third Olympics Games, second time as flagbearer for Switzerland. So I think that was maybe the highlight - entering the Bird's Nest with the flag in my hand with the whole Swiss delegation following me. So that was definitely the big thrill, next to winning the Olympic gold. I'm happy Rafa allowed me to win the doubles, I allowed him to win the singles [laughter]. I'm very happy for both of us with gold medals around our necks. It was a very, very good experience for both of us."

Nadal: "For me it was the first time there. I enjoyed meeting a lot of sportsmen. It was an amazing experience. And being there in the (athlete's) village - I make a lot of friends."

Question: If you weren't a tennis player what career path do you think you would have chosen?

Nadal: "For me, it's football, here soccer. I love that sport. I played soccer before tennis. I started when I was three years old. I have to stop because my family give me (rule) that I have to study. So I have to study. So tennis and soccer - it's impossible at that age (to do both). So finally I decide tennis."

Federer: "I want to be a boxer [laughter]. (Don King immediately chimes in, "Sign him up!"). I'm just kidding. I'm happy without a contact sport, especially with Rafa's biceps. So I'll also be in sports somewhere. My second passion is also soccer."

Question: What inspires you now at this point in your career?

Nadal: "For me, it's very easy. I always have one person in front of me. Better than me in everything. So when I see Roger in front of me all the time - better forehand, better backhand, better serve...(the audience makes a polite sound of almost disbelief). No, but believe me, that's the truth."

Federer: "For me it's really been trying to stay on top. All the challenges that I've had over the years with Agassi and Hewitt and Roddick, you name 'em, and now Rafa. I think this is definitely one of the great, great rivalries. He's definitely been the one that's been pushing me the hardest, to improve as a player, to stay ahead of him. He got me in the end and obviously I'm gonna try to get it back."

My interview with Don King moments later, about Federer and Nadal...

Question: Roger vs. Rafa - what brings you here for this?

Don King: "The U.S. Open here, with these two guys, more importantly, they want to stimulate the excitement of the game and bring people back into the fold. And who better can do it than these champions, you got Roger Federer and Rafael Nadal. It makes me feel good to have the opportunity to push greatness. To me it was for the city of New York and that's what's really meaningful to me, from Harlem to Brooklyn to all of the five boroughs all around this city. They talk about Michael Bloomberg and his great leadership as mayor, that brings people together for upward mobility and elevating blacks and whites alike, working together. Working together works. And that's what we have here. There's a lot of symbolism here. And you have two great athletes that nobody can complain about, both of them are fierce competitors. And then to bring this into New York and then into Ashe Stadium - it had all the embodiments that I just, I'm in it, gung ho."

Question: Did you see the epic Wimbledon final? What did you think of that match?

Don King: "The greatest tennis match ever between these two guys. And after five years reigning as the tennis champion and Roger, the youngster comes up, it's almost like 'The Rumble In The Jungle.' You got the two greatest athletes of all time, Muhammad Ali and George Foreman, everybody thought Ali was a little over the age and it was gonna get him. And then Ali goes out there and then he beats Foreman. That doesn't mean Rafa is gonna beat Roger - Roger's been the older in this group - he's 26, the other is 22. But the competition is there. The dubious and the doubt is there."

"You'll automatically say maybe Rafa should go out there and get him because Rafa is now at the top of his game and Rafa is doing this and the other. But nobody can stop the competitiveness of a Roger, who would be the Muhammad Ali. So would he do the 'rope a dope' with the tennis racquet? Or will George Foreman come through with that hard, rough, fierce play, that's ambidextrous, that can play left-handed or right-handed? That can punch and can knock holes in walls, like a Tyson."

"What do you have here? You got that combustion called humanity, people coming together, and really motivating and inspiring. And no one can take a back seat. You can't take a breath to go out and get a pop or a soda. You got to stay there and watch because one of the points is going to be smashing through. You don't want to miss it."

Question: Who would win a boxing match between Roger and Nadal? For a prize of $5,000,000 with Don King promoting it?

Don King: "You know what? That would be exciting. Because you have such competitors. It would be the one that wants it the most. That would be a battle of the wills, not the skills. The one who wants it the most. That can take the sacrifice and the pain for the game. The verdict is out on that one. The people would have to wait and see. I will be one of the fans that are sitting there."

"Roger squeezed my hand and said he wanted to fight. Oh baby, so it's really great, I'm excited by that. That's a great idea."

Question: You could make a fortune off a Nadal-Federer title fight. What an event it could be.

Don King: "Let me. Let me talk to them, to see what they would do and then really what they should do is donate it to charity. Give it to charity. Make it a celebrity boxing affair. And let's give the money to charity to help those who are downtrodden and denied. That's something to think about."

"In this corner, weighing in at 188 pounds, the reigning French Open champ, No. 1 in the world from Manacor, Mallorca, Spain...RAFAEL NADAL!. And weighing in at 187 pounds, the defending Wimbledon champion, No. 2 ranked challenger, from Basel, Switzerland, ROGER FEDERER!"

At the peak of their rivalry, I created a just-for-fun, magazine feature asking various tennis world figures who they would pick in a "Winner-take-all," $10-million, 12-round boxing match at Madison Square Garden...Rafael Nadal or Roger Federer. The responses were interesting, amusing and insightful...

Bud Collins: "Well I think Nadal would be too big of a left hooker with those muscles. Yeah, I think it would be Nadal. (By TKO?) No, he'd knock him out [smiles]."

Tommy Robredo: "Federer. For the age. He's five years older. When you have five more years than the other one you have a little more power, no?"

Olivier Rochus: "Nadal. He has more fighting spirit and I think physically he's stronger than Federer."

Jarkko Nieminen: "I don't know. They're both strong guys. It's tough to say. Who has better techniques. And Nadal seems to have bigger muscles but Federer has great technique in tennis. So maybe he would have the same in boxing too. So then it's about toughness."

Fernando Vicente: "Nadal, no? Nadal. Too powerful."

Justin Gimelstob: "I would say I think Nadal's one of the strongest guys on the Tour. But boxing I think has a lot more to do with than just strength. But Nadal would be rough. I don't think a lot of guys would want to have to deal with him."

Mike Agassi: "Nadal is the physically stronger man. You can see the muscle."

Vince Spadea: "Well I'd say Federer. Federer probably has more punching power and he can still move. He can stick and move."

Ivan Ljubicic: "Oh, definitely Nadal. He's stronger physically."

Carlos Moya: "Boxing...oh I guess Rafael looks stronger than Feddy but...probably the one who has been fighting more would win. I know Rafael never fought in his life [smiles] but I don't know about Federer, what he did when he was younger."

Fabrice Santoro: "The easy selection would be to say Nadal. Because he has a lot of punch and a lot of energy. But Roger is a smart athlete, a smart guy, so he would have a chance too."

Robby Ginepri: "I've never seen them without racquets in their hand against each other. I think Nadal would have a little bit more of an advantage, he's more cut up than Federer. I don't know. It'd be a fun match to see though."

Tim Henman: "I think Nadal would win. (TKO?) I think so, yeah. Great question [smiles]."

Brad Gilbert: "Nadal. He's a little bit stronger. Federer would have to keep his distance. He'd have to stick and move. I think Nadal would have to get in on the inside. He'd be more of a brawler. I don't know. But I'd pay $50 to see it [smiles]."

George Bastl: "I think Nadal. He would have more punch."

Greg Rusedski: "I think it's pretty one-sided. I think Nadal would win the boxing match. Federer would be doing the running this time instead of vice versa [smiles]."

Tomas Berdych: "Boxing match...ah, Nadal. I think maybe he's stronger and maybe for boxing it's more important."

Lleyton Hewitt: "I don't know mate. Good question [smiles]."

Donald Young: "I don't know. It's hard to decide. Depends on the surface [smiles]."

Jonas Bjorkman: "They're different. They can't be in the same weight class. 10 or 15 kilos difference, so you can't compare a boxing match like that. It's like having Tyson and one of those light heavyweights. (But what if Federer moved up in weight and he challenged him in the ring?) Then he'd win. On class [smiles]."

Andy Murray: "Nadal. He's just stronger and maybe physically just a bit better than him. But I think Tursunov would beat Nadal [smiles]. (Tursunov is standing near us in the U.S. Open locker room.)"

Michael Llodra: "Federer. He's more crazy than Nadal. (Oh, he is?) Yeah. I know him now since long time, in juniors. Now he's a little bit cool. But I see he can be more crazy than Nadal. It's not about only the muscle. He has a small muscle and he is more crazy than everybody. And you have to be crazy when you want to fight. (Can you share an example of the craziness of Federer?) No, no, no. I say he's crazy. That's all I say [smiles]!"

Roger Federer interview after his straight-set first round win at 2008 U.S. Open over M. Gonzalez:

Q. It's been so long since you haven't been a top seed at a major. Does it feel any different for you on or off the court when you go out there as a second seed?

Roger Federer: Maybe. Look at the draw maybe a little bit different. I have to start from the bottom, but that's okay. I think it would change if I were seeded three or four, because then you don't know what section you're going to be in. One or two is always pretty much the same thing. No, the change I feel is fans are really supporting me and telling me I'm still No. 1 and still the best, You're going to be there again and stuff.

So I feel like I've got unbelievable support from the fans watching me and seeing people in the streets and stuff. It's kind of really nice.

Q. Pete spoke of that same phenomenon, that all of the years he was dominating he felt that people were always cheering against him, and once he suffered a few losses all of a sudden everyone was on his side. How do you explain that phenomenon?

Roger Federer: Well, I didn't feel it myself, to be honest. I didn't think people were cheering against me. I think I have great appeal to many fans around the world, and they have always enjoyed watching me play. I'm sure with Pete the same.

Maybe because I speak so many different languages and I'm so international I have a bit of an advantage. I'm not sure. I've maybe had it once or twice when I went to into the Australian Open in 2005 when I was such a huge favorite that people were almost amazed when I lost a set. I thought then at times they were cheering for my opponents.

Other than that, it's never really been too difficult for me. I always thought fans were really good for me, excited to see me.

Q. The reception that you received last night, the ceremony prior to the beginning of play, quite an enthusiastic reception that you received. You seemed very in control. If you could, just talk a little bit about the way you're feeling after both last night and tonight.

Roger Federer: Look, you never know what kind of a reception you're going to get, especially like last night being next to so many other legends and champions and people that inspired me as a player, as a person, and then also people who were so influential in the game, you know.

And then to walk out and almost get a bigger roar than them, it's almost a little bit uneasy. At the same time it's very nice, and I appreciate it very much, especially not being an American.

We shouldn't forget that, that they're supposed to scream for the Americans here. I guess I'm very close to their hearts by now. Took me a while to maybe win over the American crowds, but I had an incredible amount of success over here. Winning the Masters a couple of times, US Open four times in a row, every other American tournament I entered I was able to win in the past.

I think just playing so many great matches here on center court and the finals with Agassi, you know, coming through that tough crowd for instance. I think people saw how much I loved playing the game and how much I love playing

here, that this is maybe like a payback for me, a great reception.
And also again tonight, excitement seeing me play and also wanting mc to do well again and winning the big ones. I think they really tried to push me forward, which was really helpful.

Q. Are you quite pleased with the match tonight? You seemed to be in control.

Roger Federer: Yeah, I think it was a good match to start off with. Never saw my opponent before. Never saw him play obviously because I never saw him. That was the tricky part. I thought the other guy played good for the pressure he was under.
And then I went on a great roll. It was the only thing I maybe look back and it was a little bit unfortunate that I was not able to stay ahead with the break in the third set.
Other than that, I thought I really served well and I thought I moved really well for the first round, and that's positive for a start.

Q. What about your experience with Don King, the whole Grapple in the Apple?

Roger Federer: Were you there, or no? I really thought it was great. It was great for tennis. Nike is really making a big push back into tennis, I think.

Q. What do you think with the boxing?

Roger Federer: I mean, they asked me. I like it. They asked me if I was going to do it and I said sure. It's the only place I would. I wouldn't do it in London or Melbourne. But this fits this place.
It's quite crazy to play tennis in such a crazy city. I never met Don King, and I think the rivalry is at its peak right now. I thought the whole Don King thing would make it more interesting. It's great for fans. I don't regret doing it. I really thought it was great fun.

Q. Next match; do you know your opponent?

Roger Federer: I know him this much more, so...
I mean, I think I know how he looks like, but...
I saw him on the little screen. I saw them play like a few points, so that's all I really know of him. I don't know him a whole a lot more. It would have been probably easier to play Capdeville who I played here last year here in the second round. I heard they were both cramping out on the court.
He'll have two days off and he'll be fine. Probably something similar from today in terms of a player from the baseline.

Q. The atmosphere with Don King the other night, is that sort of what makes the four Grand Slams so special, is that each one really has its own unique flavor? And you cap it at the end of year with, what is the US Open and Don King and New York City and all that?

Roger Federer: Yeah, I think all the Slams are very different. I think the Australian Open starting off, you know, with a bang really. I mean, couple tournaments and right away we have a Grand Slam. I really enjoy going to the Australian Open.
It's a really far trip, but it just seems more quiet because you don't have that many guests around for everybody. It's a little bit more calm in the locker room and the lounges and everything.
The fans are great. They love tennis over there. Every time I go on court anyway it's full, so that's nice.
There's such a huge hype coming into the clay court season that the French Open is like this big tournament on clay that everybody just comes to, and it's sold out also weeks ahead. You feel that the grounds are so packed. It's quite an experience.
And then obviously Wimbledon and the US Open make it unique itself. I think night session here is one of those special moments in tennis, and so is Wimbledon with the tradition. I think those really make the four majors very unique.
But I think -- let's not also forget during the year we have a great tour with the ATP. I really also enjoy those tournaments. They're unique themselves as well.
But I'm very well aware that the majors at the moment have a very big focus.

Roger Federer interview at 2004 NASDAQ-100 Open Key Biscayne on the eve of his first ATP singles match vs. Rafael Nadal:

Q. I have one that's not directly related to the match. What are the advantages and disadvantages that you find playing without a coach?

Roger Federer: Well, I think it's difficult to answer. I think there is definitely some on each side. The negatives ones, I think you have to try to, you know, put them little bit on the sides if you are with a coach or without; the same as the positive things, you have to put them more in front. You look more at those and take them, because it makes you play better tennis. I think you will always have both ways.

Q. What are some of the pluses and the minuses?

Roger Federer: Well, I mean, totally depends what kind of person you are and what for you a coach or no coach should do, you know. So, I mean, I'm not going to start saying what is good and bad in a coach or not having a coach, so it's very difficult to say.

Q. Are you close to finding a coach?

Roger Federer: No, I'm not.

Q. What are you looking for in a coach?

Roger Federer: Well, somebody, you know, who can help my game to bring it to a better level and give me advice. That's what I'm looking for in a coach. But right now, there's nothing going on.

Q. Could you see going the whole year without a coach? Could that be a possibility?

Roger Federer: Well, obviously. If things don't work out, I'm not stressing myself out. So you never know what happens. But, you know, so far it's been all right. I know I can play an entire year without a coach, so...

Q. Is Stefanki someone you've given thought to?

Roger Federer: Let's put it this way, I've thought about many coaches. Everybody who might be a candidate crossed my mind. But really haven't been close at all to have taken any decisions.

Q. I saw you here around noon, so you've been here at least seven and a half hours at this point. You had a long wait yesterday. Can you just talk about that, just the process of waiting to play this match.

Roger Federer: Well, you get used to it as a tennis player. At the US Open, I had to wait for three days until I could play a little bit. Then I had to come off after a set. So you get used to it. Sometimes it's fun, you know, sometimes it's really boring. But we're here in a group. You can entertain yourself. You know when the matches take long, at least you're here early enough to prepare. It's all about being professional.

Q. What is your scouting report on Rafael Nadal?

Roger Federer: Luckily, I played him in doubles last week so I know a little bit more about his game than I would have. So at least I don't have to see him play anymore because I know how he plays now, and I'm looking forward. It's gonna be a good match. He's definitely one of the guys that will be around in the future.

Q. His scouting report, if he had to play you, was if he plays as well as he's capable of playing and you have a bad day, he can win. Otherwise, he says, he loses. What is your reaction to that?

Roger Federer: Well, I mean, I guess he wants to take some pressure off himself, which is kind of normal. Because maybe people expect already too much of him. I don't know, people expect him maybe to beat me on a good day, which I think is totally possible. But he's right, he should push it away from him. Tomorrow he's definitely got a chance. Today wasn't my best, and I got to improve.

Q. Can you feel the target on you, people aiming for you because you're No. 1, even more so than when you were No. 2?

Roger Federer: I feel it is more of an enjoyment, being No. 1, than, you know, feeling pressure. I think I've also shown it with my results. I really just try to, you know, while I'm No. 1 in the world, I really want to enjoy it and give as much back to the game as I can.

Q. Do you sense opponents taking more risks against you because you're No. 1?

Roger Federer: Some of them might change their games, you know, because they think that maybe playing with me from the baseline is not the best idea because then I will come to the net and they have to make the passes all day so they'd rather come in themselves. I feel they maybe play a little bit more aggressive than against other players, certain players. But I think their best, they play their game and on a good day, that's sometimes good enough.

Q. How concerned were you out there down 3-1 in the third?

Roger Federer: Very. Very concerned. I was not feeling well today. I mean, incredible winds here. So it's very difficult to play. It's tough to get the rhythm. He started to play well, I thought, in the middle of the second. So was a tough one, and I didn't think I'm gonna turn this around today.

Q. The miss-hit you had would be because of the wind primarily?

Roger Federer: Yeah, wind and fatigue and just not used to play; first day I played was yesterday. So I'm really missing, you know, to hit enough tennis balls.

Q. You had a cold or flu?

Roger Federer: Yeah, I was sick. I had a fever and threw up and those kind of things, so...

Q. And you missed your flight? You were, what, a day late coming here?

Roger Federer: No, just a couple of hours.

Q. How much practice time did you miss then?

Roger Federer: Two, three days.

Q. You have problems with your feet?

Roger Federer: No, the tape was coming off. Didn't disturb my game. But just had to take it off.

Q. What did you say to yourself at 3-1 in the third that changed everything?

Roger Federer: Well, the wind was getting stronger and stronger, you know. I didn't have my confidence on my forehand. I couldn't hit three or four balls in a row, so I felt like he was really starting to -- not to hardly miss anymore from the baseline. The beginning, you know, he was giving me a lot of easy points. I thought, "Geez, this will be very, very difficult, you know, hopefully I can just get a good start to one of those games on his service." That's what I got right away at 3-1, so, got a little fortunate today.

Q. (Inaudible)?

Roger Federer: No mistakes, tried to move and at least hold your own serve so you don't get down two breaks. But you got to hope on mistakes from the opponent.

Q. A couple days ago Andy was in chatting with us. We were talking about how difficult it is for players at the very top of the rankings to have any kind of relationship because they always want to keep a certain distance because of the competitiveness. He said, "If Roger called me up and said, 'Why don't we go out for dinner,' I'd love to do that, I'd have no problem with it." Would you?

Roger Federer: Sure (smiling). I mean, we shouldn't talk, like, in a triangle, but I agree, it is very difficult because, you know, usually we stay at different hotels or we're very busy. We've got our own, you know, people around us. I think, you know, I go out with the Swiss players; he probably goes out with the Americans or his clan. I'm talking about any player now. You know, it's a professional sport so you want to do everything just for that day so you're ready. We get along well. We never had a problem together. I could imagine myself having a drink with Andy, I have in the past so...

Q. Do you feel you would have won that kind of match like today like two years ago?

Roger Federer: Well, you never know. Obviously, I'm a better player now, mentally stronger, physically stronger. But I cannot say because last year I lost it 7-6 in the third in the quarters. But, you know, different opponent, not so much wind.

Q. You used to hate the wind when you were younger?

Roger Federer: Yeah, well, you see it. Tennis is just not as much fun as it is without because you cannot risk as much, you cannot hit the ball as hard as you want. You've got to really calculate everything you do. So that takes away a little bit of creativity, I think. I've learned to use the wind to my favor. That is important to my game.

Q. When you say that Rafael maybe wants to take pressure off himself because there are a lot of expectations on him, do you see in what he's going through maybe what you went through?

Roger Federer: Sure.

Q. Do you think, is that part of what -- maybe you see that where other people would not?

Roger Federer: Yeah, but, I think, you know, his ranking , he has already proven himself at his age, you know, to be ranked as good as he is, I think he's already actually proven that he's a great player. He doesn't right now need to beat all these top players just to show them that in three years' time he can be No. 1 in the world and win Grand Slams. I think all he needs is time, and I think he's a very quiet guy and confident on the court. I felt the same way at his age. So looking forward to playing a player like him, you know, because I think he's a good player. Tomorrow maybe I'll tell you he's a great player, but I first got to play him, so...

Rafael Nadal interview after beating World No. 1 Roger Federer 6-3 6-3 in third round of 2004 NASDAQ-100 Key Biscayne:

Q. How does it feel to beat the No. 1 seed?

Rafael Nadal: Yes, I'm very happy because I played one of the best matches in my life. Obviously, he didn't play his best tennis and that's the reason why I could win. I mean, if he had played his best tennis, I would have had no chance. But that's what happens in tennis. If a player like me plays at a very, very good level and a top player like Roger doesn't play his best tennis, I can win. But, sure, I'm really, really happy.

Q. (Inaudible)?

Rafael Nadal: Yeah, I played almost perfect tennis today because I was playing inside the court, dominating the exchanges and pressing him so he couldn't play his game. But one thing I forgot, I served extremely well today, probably I never served like this in my life. That was really the key.

Q. Everybody seems to be afraid to play Federer. You did not look like you were afraid.

Rafael Nadal: Yes, I mean, I was afraid that he could win 6-1, 6-1 or 6-1, 6-2 but I was really looking forward to playing this match because I was playing against the No. 1 player in the world. I went on court with a positive attitude, not with the attitude of, "Oh, let's try and win one game."

Q. How would you describe your playing style?

Rafael Nadal: When I play well, I'm a very aggressive player with a good forehand and I fight very hard on the court.

Q. Technically and tactically, what was the key of the match? How did you approach this match?

Rafael Nadal: Well, I knew that the most important point was that I couldn't let him play his own game, because if he can play his own game, he wins 6-1, 6-1, 6-1, 6-2 like it's happening this year and it's never happened in tennis before. So from the first point I knew that I had to dictate the exchange for him not to be able to play his game.

Q. How do you organize your day for practicing, for tactics of the matches if you are just on your own?

Rafael Nadal: No, I'm here with somebody, I'm here with Jofre Porta, who usually is with Carlos Moya, but Carlos Moya, he's here with Joan Bosch. I'm here with somebody that helps me. At the same time, before every match, I call my uncle and so we speak about the match.

Q. As you said, you served very well today. Did you change anything on your serve since last year?

Rafael Nadal: Yeah, it's mostly that every match I try to hit my serve harder, and, you know, every match I play, because I think that's how you can improve yourself; you have to be more aggressive and go for it. That's the key. Obviously, I know I've changed my movement a little bit, but that's the key, going for it more. Like, for instance, last week, I served at 6-5 against Calleri in the third set, and I didn't serve hard, I served like slowly, and I lost it. So that's the key really.

Q. The way you played tonight, it suggests that you're not the kind of player who's going to be afraid of playing on any surface, whether it's hard court, clay, even grass. Is that your goal, to be playing on all the surfaces well?

Rafael Nadal: No, I've always said that I'm the kind of player that can play well on all surfaces. I played well on grass last year. I played well on hard court outdoors. I play well on clay, obviously, because I'm used to it; I grew up on clay. And maybe I didn't play well last year indoors, but it was mostly because it was the end of the year and, you know, I was little bit tired. It was my first year, and I was a little bit tired at the end of the year. If you're not in very good shape physically and mentally, you cannot compete at this level.

Q. Last year when you lost to El Aynaoui at the US Open, you said you didn't feel you belonged to that top level of tennis and that was the reason why you had lost. What's the difference now?

Rafael Nadal: Definitely, this year I have much more confidence and I know that I can play at that level, that I belong to the higher level of players. Obviously, last year I was winning my matches because I was fighting very hard. This is the same this year, but I'm also winning because I raised my level and I believe I belong to the top.

Q. Do you think you could play that kind of level in a match in a Grand Slam tournament, the best-of-five sets?

Rafael Nadal: Well, I've only played like Wimbledon and I got to the third round, and then US Open I got to the second round and then in Australia I lost to Hewitt in three sets. So I only need to play Paris, which I haven't played before, and that's different there because it's clay courts. But I think that physically I'm not such a bad player.

Q. This is a result that's going to reverberate around the world. Do you think your mobile phone will be pretty busy with calls tonight, congratulations?

Rafael Nadal: No, not right now because it's 4 a.m. in Spain so everybody's sleeping. Tomorrow, the papers won't have this news. But, yeah, maybe Internet and on the teletext I will start getting some calls.

Q. You lost last year to Gonzalez, so what do you think about that match and tomorrow's match?

Rafael Nadal: Yeah, sure, I lost against him and it was in Stuttgart. I thought I played a good match, one of the best matches up to that point in my career. It was the first time that I played against somebody who hit the ball so hard. He was doing everything. I was just running around. I played well to win the second set, and then I lost in three sets. But I think tomorrow is going to be different because now I'm used to these kind of players.

Q. Your win today and Monaco's win over Guga yesterday were the same matches - you showed you're young players, hitting the ball very hard and dominating the other players. Is that the tennis of the future, and if your style of play doesn't work, do you have anything else to fall back on?

Rafael Nadal: Well, I don't think that Monaco or I discovered the world, because that's actually the way tennis players are playing right now, like Ferrero, Moya, Federer, Safin, you know, hitting the ball very hard. I'm particularly happy for Monaco because he's played well this year, especially in Buenos Aires and Brazil and here. I've known him quite well because he was training in Spain, so I've known him since the time he was playing futures in Spain.

Q. How important was it for you to play Davis Cup this year? How did it help you believe you are part of the top players?

Rafael Nadal: Yeah, it's true. Davis Cup was one of the best, if not the best experience so far. I was there, I lost my first two points, and then I won the last and it was just unbelievable. Obviously, now we have this match coming up in Mallorca. I would like to play again. But in Spain we have a lot of good players - Ferrero, Moya, who are ahead of me. I'm hoping to play maybe in the doubles, but the team is going to be announced on Tuesday.

Roger Federer interview after losing match to Rafael Nadal at 2004 NASDAQ-100 Key Biscayne:

Q. Your thoughts on the match? What was he able to do to get you out of rhythm?

Roger Federer: Well, I think it's always difficult to play someone for the first time, first of all. But I think, you know, overall he played a very good match. He was the better player today. It was tough for me to, you know -- I mean, I had time to get the rhythm, but, you know, he played very aggressive and I couldn't quite play maybe the way I wanted to.

Q. Were you surprised how aggressive he did come out? It seemed like every shot he was hitting was perfect.

Roger Federer: He doesn't hit the ball flat and hard. It's more with a lot of spin, which makes the ball bounce, bounce high, and that's a struggle I had today. I tried to get out of it, but kind of couldn't. I thought in the beginning I maybe wasn't going for my shots enough, where in the end I thought I was hitting the ball better. But I felt the match maybe kind of went his way, and, you know, he hit some really incredible shots. That's what youngsters do, so... (Laughter).

Q. Are you surprised such a young guy could come at you like that?

Roger Federer: No, no, I'm not surprised. I've heard a lot about him and saw some matches of him. I think this is not a big surprise for everybody.

Q. You played a lot of tennis this year already. Do you feel more tired physically or mentally?

Roger Federer: My fatigue right now has got nothing to do with all the matches I've played this year. I've been sick, and this was my problem for the imperfect preparation for this tournament. Yesterday I was (going) a lot in the wind. Today I played against a player who was just better. That was my problem for this week. Now I have time to rest and prepare for Davis Cup.

Q. Do you feel better physically than yesterday, or do you feel the same?

Roger Federer: Different. I had a lot of pain in my whole body from the match of yesterday because I couldn't prepare the way I wanted to. But, you know, I didn't feel as tired as yesterday. But tough to explain. Just, you know, I felt what was missing today was just the reactions and maybe the fight in the corners which were not the same than maybe I'm used to.

Q. What do you think is the biggest weapon Nadal has?

Roger Federer: I think his forehand, you know, is for sure his biggest shot in his game, and his all-court speed.

Q. It wasn't long ago you were 17. Can you imagine playing with that attitude against the No. 1 player in the world?

Roger Federer: Was it not good?

Q. It was great. His attitude today, I mean. Could you imagine you at 17 years old...

Roger Federer: Well, we have to get a tape when I played Moya, Moya in Marseille when I was 17. But I think, you know, he's a different character on the court. He relies much more on his fighting spirit, like Lleyton does a little bit, you know, I compare him at his age. So, you know, everyone has their attitude. I think it's a definite good one to have very much success early in his career.

Q. As the world No. 1, still only 22, does it frighten you that he is almost five years younger than you?

Roger Federer: Well, what can you do (smiling)? I think he's put a lot of hard work into his game. We all know that, you know, the youngsters from today - because we feel young, but there's always younger players than you, and, you know, we all remember when we were 17, we already felt we were great players. Then suddenly, you're around for a few years and you feel like, "Well, now I've proven it to everybody I'm a good player." It's totally different view of the game, especially I think interesting are the first three years. So I think he's enjoying his tennis. That's exactly what he should do. We'll see how strong he will be in two years. But, I mean, the start to his career so far has been incredible.

Q. Did you sense that he was nervous at all? Did you see that in him?

Roger Federer: No. In the beginning maybe little bit, when you walk on court. I think he's kind of a little bit shy, you know, on court. He looks at me as an incredible great player, you know. I just felt more of a respect level than nerve.

Q. I guess this win for him tonight must feel, in a way, like it felt for you when you beat Sampras, that sort of major victory, that major breakthrough. How important is that kind of victory to your career?

Roger Federer: For me, it was -- I think it's -- I don't know if you can compare. Mine was in Wimbledon, you know. Definitely this is also big tournament, but, I don't know, it's tough because I'm still not much, much older than he is. Sampras, for me, was more of -- I think more than I am for him. He's got different idols, I think (smiling). For me, I think this win counts little bit different for us.

Q. How will you prepare for the Davis Cup?

Roger Federer: How I will prepare? The way we always do (smiling).

Q. When do you go to Switzerland?

Roger Federer: I don't know when I'm leaving, when I'm arriving to the team. They started practicing on Monday, which is tomorrow. They will start the practice tomorrow, and I will join them when I get back to Switzerland. So when that will be, I don't know.

Q. Do you think the heat stroke that you got in Indian Wells, although you've got a thick head of black hair, do you think of wearing a cap in those conditions perhaps next time?

Roger Federer: It's a good point which I thought about. But it's really the first time I've experienced something like this. I've played in some heat in my career. So, I mean, I'll try to continue playing the way I did. If I will get it a second time, then I'll put even more thoughts into it (laughter)... and start playing with a cap, thanks to you (laughter).

Q. What's closest to your heart - to win Davis Cup or the Gold Medal in the Olympics this year?

Roger Federer: Olympics would mean more to me.

Q. Do you go with any particular plan today and you couldn't make it happen, or you went just to see? Considering that you do not have a coach right now and you're coaching yourself, how did you prepare for the match in this case?

Roger Federer: Well, I think the difficulty was that I've never played him, so that makes it more difficult. He's a young player who takes, you know -- you never know what he will do next because he's very unpredictable. He will suddenly take a lot of risks. That's what he sometimes did and surprised me. So for me, you know, it was important to, you know, to try to play aggressive. But I felt, you know, the conditions were very slow out there and maybe lost a little bit of my confidence in the early -- beginning of the match. I came to the net a few times and missed my chances there. He passed me well. So this is actually when maybe already I started to lose a little bit, you know, of confidence, when the match went his way. I started to take more chances from the baseline and maybe I played a little bit too much from the baseline with him instead of maybe coming to the net more. It's definitely got something to do with his game as well; he didn't allow me to. That's the way he played.

Q. How do you think you'll do at the French Open on clay this year?

Roger Federer: Myself?

Q. Uh-hmm.

Roger Federer: Long way to go. I don't know. Looking forward to it, you know. I can only do better than the last two years. I didn't win a set, so... (Laughing). My goal is to do better and hopefully win a round. But I've proven in the past on clay, you know, it can also work out for me. It's definitely one of the -- I have high hopes in the French Open this year.

Chapter 7: Random Roger Stuff

Annette Bremner (Tennis Fan): "I saw both matches in Indian Wells in which Blake defeated Nadal in the semi, and the next afternoon, in which Federer defeated Blake in the final. They were astounding matches. When Blake gave his finalist speech, he referenced his accident in Rome, when he cracked a vertebrae when he hit a net post. He said he'd received one card from a fellow player, and that player was Roger Federer. The stadium audience applauded; Roger just nodded a quiet acknowledgement and smiled."

The Federer-Fish Practice Session On Arthur Ashe Stadium, August 25, 2011:

It's about 1:30 and I'm supposed to meet my friend Yeonah at 2 in front of Ashe so I enter the Stadium to see who's using the court...and it's Roger Federer and Mardy Fish. And there are only about ten scattered people watching. They must've just started because they're hitting from the baseline and it's still light hitting.

Roger is focused as always and doesn't talk so much during the workout but Fish is more vocal. He says, "Sorry Rog," twice after misses. And, "Nice shot Rog," after a sweet stroke.

It's rather windy today. Fish comments to himself, I think, "This wind is bad."

They take breaks every ten minutes or so and sit down together on the chairs to the right of the umpire stand. Their coaches and entourage guys – Severin Luthi, Paul Annacone, David Nainkin, and a few others I don't recognize, stand around them respectfully as they chat. All I can think of is, wow, these guys are just as in awe of Fish and Federer as us onlookers. To be among the top 10 players in the world at the sport of tennis...these guys are simply marvels sitting on their blue and white wooden thrones.

It's very windy today on the court and at one break time, Federer mentions a match where it was really windy and he tells a story about it but I can't quite hear all the details. Then Fish shares a tennis/wind-related memory.

They change sides, Fish comments, "Now I'm on the good side."

Annacone instructs what he wants to be done and the Fish team complies easily. They play a game to 15, where the returner of the feed has to hit an attack shot and go to the net. They alternate who feeds who first. Fish jumps out to a 5-2 lead but Fed soon levels it at 5. Roger hits a vintage forehand winner down the line and adds a "Come on!" for an explanation point. He doesn't really smile when he says it, he's surprisingly serious. It's as if the great one's ultra-competitive juices flow, even in simple practice drills like this. It's light-hearted but critical at the same time. Hitting shots like that are still thrilling, even for a champion like Federer.

Fish then connects on a forehand crosscourt winner passing shot by Roger with no more than two inches of net clearance. Roger smiles and says," Whaaaaat??!"

Then Roger hits a perfect winning backhand volley and states, "That's a South African," but I'm not sure why. Fish clearly likes the brilliance of the shot and quickly adds, "Rafter."

Fish is savoring this session of hitting with the Great Federer, the reverence and respect is so apparent to the eye and ear, and the tone of voice he speaks to him with. It's almost like he's hosting Roger at his home and he goes out of his way to entertain the court master.

Fish ends up winning the game to 15.

After the last shot before the next rest, Federer holds the ball and pretends to shoot it as a basketball as he flips it toward the net. Fish notices this and replies, simply, "Kobe."

Then as they sit down together, Fish senses a cue and begins to discuss basketball. "Sharapova's guy Sasha Vujucic, is a really nice guy," he says, before launching into a story about some hooper from Stanford who played pro in Europe and Fed listens, quite clearly enjoying the company of Fish. I can't hear all of what Fish talks about. Then Fish changes the topic and begins to talk about K-Swiss, their offices in California – I believe he said Thousand Oaks. Fish explains to Roger how K-Swiss has "two players in the top ten now, me and Monfils." But I can hear he pronounces Monfils as "Mon-fills."

Fish seems very pleased with K-Swiss as he describes how open-minded the company is to suggestions and innovations. He says you can give K-Swiss any shorts you like and ask them to make them similar. You can also give them a material you like and they will use the same fabric. You tell them you play better in them and they listen. It was very interesting to hear Fish sing the praises of his attire company to Roger Federer, who as we all know wears Nike.

The last conversation I heard was about some kind of feed ball tournaments they hold, I believe in California. Nainkin explained it but I couldn't quite hear the details, from my seat by the right baseline side. Fish adds, "Gavin (Rossdale) plays, Gavin plays."

Nainkin remarks, with a smile, "Guys miss feeds sometimes."

Fish adds again, "Spadea won it. Ten grand to win."

But it's about 2 now. I have to leave the court and leave Fed and Fish to go meet my friend.

One year later Federer and Fish practice again before the start of the 2012 U.S. Open. Both enter Louis Armstrong stadium court in early afternoon to an enormous applause which is obviously directed at the man from Switzerland. A smiling Fish shows his sense of humor and raises his arms playfully to acknowledge the crowd roar which is clearly for his buddy Federer.

Justyna Wereszka: "On the Friday before the 2012 U.S. Open started, there was a kids clinic at the indoor courts facility. Roger was scheduled to make an appearance there. I was volunteering at this event and we expected Roger to show up and maybe stay for a few minutes and leave. But he stayed for an hour and fifteen minutes and played with the kids on the court. He was having a lot of fun playing and smiling with the kids. We were surprised he stayed for so long and had so much fun."

Gavin Rossdale Interview at 2010 U.S. Open:

Musician and friend of Federer, Gavin Rossdale was at the outdoor area of the U.S. Open player's lounge this year on a sunny afternoon and he was kind enough to sit down and discusses his love of tennis...

"I grew up playing tennis and just loving it. I used to get a kick out of watching Wimbledon. I think that Wimbledon is a big deal for most British kids. I never thought that I'd end up one day watching a friend of mine play in the final on Center Court, but that's exactly what happened. I first met Roger through a mutual friend in New York about six or seven years ago and we've since become good friends. Roger is super cool and he has so much respect for everyone. I think that people connect with that quality in him."

"I like to watch players with flair. Roger, obviously, but almost everyone in the top 100 is pretty good. There are no duds. The athleticism of the top guys is phenomenal. You get the feeling that they could excel in any sport. There's a real intense artistry in tennis though, and there's so much passion and commitment. I enjoy the game and appreciate it for what it is."

"Of the younger players, I like to watch Ernests Gulbis. Gulbis is a particularly striking player – a crusher. And I think Gael Monfils has lots of potential. I like Andy Murray too. He reminds me a little of John McEnroe. He's got such great hands and he just sweeps up everything with his returns. He's an incredibly gifted tennis player and I like his attitude too. Also, the fact that I'm half Scottish makes me especially happy when he does well."

"I love taking part in pro-am tournaments such as Chrissie Evert's event in Boca Raton. Those events are a great thrill, not only because we get to play in front of large crowds of people but also I get to play in more competitive matches. I've played against a lot of good players in those tournaments – Jim Courier, Tommy Haas, Lindsay Davenport, Corina Morariu, Justin Gimelstob, Luke and Murphy Jensen. The downside is the collective groan you hear when you screw up – that's a tough sound for me. It's worse than being out of tune [laughs]."

"I play as much as I can when I'm not in the studio or touring. I often find myself playing against professionals, people like Wade McGuire, Mark Philippoussis, Vince Spadea and Sam Querrey. Sam's a friend, he's great, he comes to my house and plays. It's not like I'm going to be able to beat these guys, so my goal is to hit properly and keep up with them the best I can. I'm competitive with myself, so I try to do things right. I don't hit and giggle, I have fun by being intense."

"The biggest appeal of tennis for me is that it's one on one. Almost gladiatorial. Doubles is great too, but you can't beat the feeling that everything is down to you."

"The strength of my game is that I'm pretty athletic. So stamina is the key for me. I do a lot of off court training. Pilates is amazing. I do all the stuff like strength work, lunges. I used to think that playing was just enough, but I've changed my mind on that."

Wimbledon 2002 Mario Ancic after beating Federer in the first round:

Q. Congratulations. How do you feel now?

Mario Ancic: I'm feeling -- I feel great. I just play one of the best matches in my life, so how can I feel? I cannot feel better I think.

Q. Was it a surprise to you?

Mario Ancic: I came first time to play Centre Wimbledon, they put me on Centre Court for my first time. I qualified, I had nothing to lose. I was just confidence. I knew I could play. I'm young. I believe in myself and I just go out there and try to do my best. Just I didn't care it who did I play, it doesn't matter. I just went there and play.

Q. Did you know anything about Roger? You had a special game plan or had spoken to Mr. Ivanisevic to see what you could do?

Mario Ancic: Yeah, actually I spoke with him yesterday. And just I knew him from TVs. Some time I play Key Biscayne. That was my only big tournament this year. Otherwise I was in challengers. But I knew already how is he playing. I don't know that he knew how I'm playing, but that was my advantage. And, yeah, I knew I didn't have any tactics, just I was playing, enjoying.

Q. How close are you to Goran? What does he mean to you?

Mario Ancic: We are from same town. When I was growing up, he was in Split and we always hit, even when I was 10. We were in Davis Cup together, we play in Olympics, doubles. I know he was always good to me. Sometimes I felt like he was my bigger brother in tournaments, and I know I can always relate on him.

Like yesterday when I call him about tactics, you know. He's a great guy and also player as you saw last year.

Q. How upset was he not to be here himself when he spoke to you yesterday?

Mario Ancic: I think he cannot watch too much other guys playing. He just sitting there. That's his character. But his arm is like -- it's not so great. He's now doing exercise. I hope and I think we all hope he come better next year.

Q. What did he exactly tell you yesterday as tips on how to play Federer? What did he tell you?

Mario Ancic: He told me just he has great forehand, just stay away from him. He can serve good, but sometimes just attack him on second. He knows to, like, make pressure on my second so I have to be little bit aggressive with that one. And, you know, he was mostly slicing backhand, sometimes hitting it. But I knew there was my chance. And I was serving good today.

Q. You had a chance last week to hit with Jim Courier. Did that help you in any way? Did he give you any advice or tips on your game?

Mario Ancic: Yeah, it was a great experience to hit with him. We spoke about my game. We hit for one hour. He's still hitting good, I can tell you that (laughter). And, no, he just told me play my game just be relaxed. And that's it.

Wimbledon 2002 Roger Federer interview after losing in the first round to Mario Ancic:

Q. How devastating is this loss today? Was there a reason?

Roger Federer: Well, still looking for reasons why, yes, why I played so bad. I'm terribly down right now. I mean, it's quite normal after such a loss. And I expected much more than coming in here and losing in straight sets. So I'm very disappointing. For the moment, I haven't got any words.

Q. Did you know him? I think on the tour, everybody knew he was a little bit of a threat, was considered a big talent. Did you know about his game?

Roger Federer: I mean, I don't know. I knew he was young, but I didn't know much more. I tried to get some information from other players. I mean, a lot of guys hit with him. I never did. But I got my information, and I just couldn't really figure out his game today. My game let him play well today. So didn't really matter actually the way he played. I'm just really down about my game today. That was quite bad.

Q. How surprised were you that he was able to maintain his level over those three sets?

Roger Federer: Yeah, I mean, I just had my chances, you know. In the second set, I missed them. Okay, maybe in the first one I have the break. I couldn't take my chances today. I had Love-40 in the second. This was really my only big chance throughout the whole match, and I didn't take it. He deserves to be through because I just couldn't come up with the right shots at the right moment. And that hurts especially in a Grand Slam over five sets where I really think I'm the better player. But today it was just too bad.

Q. What caused you most problems against him?

Roger Federer: Well, I couldn't quite figure out his serve. I was struggling to read his toss. Other than that, I mean, he returns pretty good. But I just felt like from the beginning on, I was not serving well. Tried to get more serves in. But as soon as I wanted to go for an ace, I will never make it. I still think the conditions are much slower than last year somehow. I mean, just I haven't looked at the stats, but I maybe made one ace, I think. I mean, it's a joke if I think I made 25 against Pete last year or something. I don't know what was wrong today. My serving was, for sure, not very good.

Q. You mentioned Pete. Obviously you scored one of the biggest upsets in recent years. Now to suffer this upset.

Roger Federer: It hurts. I mean, I was looking forward a lot to this tournament again just because I was so happy that I heard I was playing on Centre Court. It's a special place out here. I think it's the best centre court in the world and I love playing on it. After nice experiences, even against Henman, I thought it was a nice match. To come out today and play such tennis I played today, it's just a shocker. So I'm very disappointed. It's going to take some time until I get over it, but I will have to work hard and come back strong for the American hard courts.

Q. Roland Garros and now Wimbledon. Is there a problem with you being the favorite? Do you have a problem in Grand Slam tournaments?

Roger Federer: No. Usually I prefer to be in the favored role. But I still think Arazi was a very tough opponent at the French Open. Here, I mean, usually I should win this match. I'm high favorite over Ancic. He played well today. Yeah, this is very disappointing to lose back to back first round in Grand Slams. I'm looking for reasons why, but I have time to figure that out, so we'll see.

(www.asapsports.org)

Chapter 8: Federer Fan Perspectives

Amir Zaman: "Everyone expects Federer to win against all and that's pressure on him which does not allow him to showcase his full natural talent. Whereas the players opposite to him, do not feel the same pressure as like Fed, because if they lose against Fed, it is taken as expected. Federer showed his true ability and his unmatched variety. Federer is the only player in the entire history who plays with single hand and shows such a range of shots and has been successful at the highest level for so many years. He does not look as threatening physically as Nadal or Tsonga but despite his silken frame, his services are unmatched. Undoubtedly the most graceful and natural athelete, the tennis sport has ever seen is Roger and Roger only! I doubt any one will come close to Roger in the future! You lose or you win and we love you."

Ibrahim Kashoor: "I would just like to state something that is really not important. I don't know if you watched the coin toss (of Federer vs. Murray 2013 Australian Open SF). There was a little kid taking photos with the two players and tossing the coin. I would like to point out how Roger Federer helped orient the kid while taking pictures and even said something to him when the kid was leaving the court (probably a thank you or a well done) while Andy Murray completely ignored the little fellow. Now I'm not judging Andy because he is obviously thinking about the match and not paying attention to anything around him, including the little kid. All I want to say after all this talk is that these little things are what make us love Roger. His manners and behaviors are those of noble human not just an elite player. These little things are the reason I'm not going to be watching tennis as regularly as I do know after Roger retires.
Finally I would like to congratulate Roger for reaching this far at the Australian Open and wish the best for Murray against Novak in the finals but most importantly I would like to thank Roger for simply being who he is. He is truly something that will never happen to this sport again."

Joan Leslie: "Roger you are the darling of two old ladies in Durban, South Africa. I'm 79 and my friend is 76. I'm sure we are your greatest fans in the whole world. We've been watching you like forever and are holding thumbs that you will win this Australian Open. We send you much love and best wishes."

Helen Marshall: "I feel very lucky and privileged to live in the era of the greatest player of all time - Roger Federer. An all-around true sportsman and gentleman on and off court! A delight to watch, a shining example to all up-and-coming players and without him tennis would be much the poorer. This man is a genius - an often over-used term but completely applicable to Roger."

Vo Trung Hieu: "Mr. Roger Federer is legend of tennis, who let me know tennis and love it."

Jimmy Connors: "In an era of specialists – you're either a clay court specialist, a grass court specialist or a hard court specialist... or you're Roger Federer."

Kamila Sadvakasova: "Tennis means Federer. He is the number one. And he will be the best forever."

Gerard Onyiuke "The imperious Roger Federer! So sublime... unquestionably a deity in the game...even if he gets beat, his conquerors would still wish they had a bit of him in them."

Donald Kramer: "Roger Federer is truly class act...makes me proud to be a tennis player!"

Monica Oncescu: "Roger is the best player and will remain the best no matter of the results. His class will never be surpassed."

Joan Strassman: "Thank you for all the pleasure I've had from watching you -- in my 78 years, you are the best I have ever seen; your combination of skill, poetry in motion and thought make you the absolute example of how the game should be played. Again, I thank you, and always hope I can watch you again."

Philip Griffiths: "To me Roger Federer is what the game of tennis is all about, not only in the way he plays but in his professionalism and impeccable manners. He is the whole package and what the young, up and coming tennis players should aspire to as a role model. The only other player that has ever enthralled me like him is the great Bjorn Borg. Thanks Roger - tennis won't be the same for me if you're not there!"

Peter Frybort: "Even though I am a Nole Fan, Federer has not only achieved a lot in his career, but next to all his wins and titles he's also a 'real' gentleman and he is also very likable, so he will remain one of the greatest champions ever."

Jeng Roque: "Win or lose, ROGER FEDERER is STILL the GREATEST TENNIS PLAYER OF ALL TIME! He has nothing to prove anymore!"

Chapter 9: Media And Insider Perspectives

Various tennis insiders share their personal insights and encounters with Roger Federer. In this chapter you will learn in detail about Federer's excellence in dealing with the media from an ATP VP, amusing chance encounters with Roger at the washroom sink and Ocean Drive in South Beach, and much more...

Amelie Mauresmo: "I think my first memory of Roger was when he beat Pete Sampras at Wimbledon. I think it was in 2001, last 16. And we see this young guy coming up and beating, at the time, the master of Wimbledon. And the way he did it, the talent and also the emotions that he showed at the end, with respect."

Question: Ever hit with, meet or have a conversation with Roger?

Amelie Mauresmo: "Not hit, I meet him yeah, two times. Nothing special. Yeah...sharing the Champions Dinner at Wimbledon with him was quite special. And fun. And exciting."

Question: Lasting memory of him for you, on court or off?

Amelie Mauresmo: "That's tough. On the court but also off the court...he's quite a character, which doesn't really show on the court. That he's funny. He laughs all the time. Likes to tease people and I like that [smiles]."

Nima Naderi (www.Tennisconnected.com): "I first saw Federer play live at the 2000 Masters Series event in Toronto. His opponent was Lleyton Hewitt. At the time, Hewitt had won their first two meetings and was on course to take seven of the next nine encounters. Although Federer lost that match to Hewitt in three sets after winning the first, the ease and fluidity in which he struck the ball was like nothing I've ever seen before. He wore a baseball cap back then and not his famous bandanna, but his elegant strokes and quiet footwork were ever present. It was evident that he played the game with much more ease than the other players, but he remained explosive and intent on improving. In a way, he had so many shots, that it took him a while to figure out how to use everything in his arsenal."

Richard Williams (Father/Coach of Venus & Serena Williams): "My first memory of Federer...I remember at Wimbledon and some girl from Sweden came to me and asked what I'd thought he'd become, how do I think he would do? But I said I'd never seen him play. I don't know, let's give him time and we'll find out how he'll do. That way I wouldn't make a mistake [laughs]. But I think he turned out to be one of the greatest players there is. And I have a TON of respect for him. Certainly, I think he was one of the players that played unhurt all the time. I think he's gonna be one of the greatest of all time. If I had to vote for him I would vote that he would be."

Question: Lasting memory of Roger, on or off court?

Richard Williams: "I would say off the court. I think he's so nice and friendly to everyone that it's unbelievable. But I think if he was a rough guy, I think he would keep winning for the next three or four years. He has enough. But some players are just good. Some players are rough and tough - like Andre Agassi and Marcelo Rios. Roger is not what you call a rough/tough player. He's a nice, smooth player. Something like Pete Sampras. But if you have a rough player, that looks you in the eye and they don't give a damn about you one way or the other. And they don't apologize when they beat you. That's the last thing I think he needs. And I think that's what could make him win majors the next two or three years if he had to."

Question: How are your personal relations with Roger?

Richard Williams: "I always thought it was a great relationship, in my opinion. We talked some, we talked in the locker room a lot. Laughed. I just think he's a great player. Talked to some of his coaches he worked with. I think he's a terrific human being. Gracious. Friendly. But he's a great player."

Nicola Arzani (ATP Senior Vice President, Public Relations & Marketing)

Question: How do the amount of media demands for Roger Federer compare to other players?

Nicola Arzani: "Well, I would say that Roger was probably the first No. 1 player on the ATP World Tour that got there, having started his career under the ATP Stars program which we introduced at the end of the 1990s, for the pro players to give back more. Just before that we only had press conferences as a mandatory commitment for the players during the event. And then we introduced the ATP Stars program at the end of the 1990s and under the Stars program, each player in the main draw of a tournament has to give two hours of their time to promotions, for a maximum of two hours during the week. So Roger was probably the first No. 1 to have done this his whole career with the Stars program. He was always available and he gave more than the two hours, like week in and week out. And also the fact that he speaks not only English but French and German. And basically everywhere he goes around to, they almost treat him like one of their own players. That has really added to the amount of activities that he has done throughout his career."

Question: Take a week in general. What does a typical week in media demands look like for Roger?

Nicola Arzani: "Well, it's difficult to say. But in terms of media requests after every match, I would say eight to ten including TV. And before the tournament everybody wants to have a little bit of time with him one-on-one. I would say, considering he plays about 80 matches a year, it's been close to 60-80 hours doing press after the match. And if you go through the pre-tournament and special features, one-on-one interviews, then I would say he did go over the 100 hours, only for media."

Question: Do you remember an abnormally busy week of demands for Roger?

Nicola Arzani: "Even like the last tournament he played in Indian Wells (2013) was quite easy for him. He played Dubai - he helped us launch the ATP Heritage program with Novak Djokovic. Then he had a photo shoot, then he had two one-on-one interviews, then he had the media day. Then he had the player party. I mean, already he went over the two hours by far, in Indian Wells as well, as he did the ATP photo shoot, he did the media, he did the ground-breaking for the new stadium with Larry Ellison. So just taking the last couple of tournaments - Rotterdam he did almost like a full day of promotions in town - appearance/autograph session, TV shows. He almost had like an entire day before he played his first match promoting the tournament in Rotterdam, outside the tournament venue. So definitely, he's already gone above and beyond the commitment."

Question: Sounds like he's done almost as many interviews as ATP matches.

Nicola Arazni: "Well, it's difficult to count. Sometimes it's funny, after he won a Grand Slam, he had spent more time doing media that same night and the following day than he spent on the court. I mean, he's been the greatest ambassador. And I would say not only for tennis but I don't believe any other sportsman at that level has spent as much time promoting and helping the sport. Because you see the media side, the promotional side, but you have to remember, he's been the President of the ATP Player Council for the last five or six years, giving countless hours to the meetings, conference calls. He's been instrumental behind a lot of different programs of development for the ATP. So along with the media and promotion side, there's also the political or leadership roles that he's had in tennis for a number of years now. It's been amazing. He's always said that he wants to leave tennis in better shape when he retires. And he does everything possible to improve the game for everyone involved."

Question: Has Roger's example had a positive influence on other top players like Nadal, Djokovic, Murray and their relations with the media?

Nicola Arzani: "I believe so yes, because they saw him at the top doing so many things and promoting the game and they just followed him in his footsteps. First Rafa, then Novak and now Andy, I mean, they're all fantastic to work with. They had Roger as an example. When they started breaking through when Roger was No. 1 and doing so much for tennis, I remember Rafa and Nole were part of the Player Council at one stage. So they got involved as well. Those four guys have done a lot together, also off the court, together with the ATP and the ATP Player Council to improve a lot of things."

Question: Please share a lasting memory of working with Federer?

Nicola Arzani: "I've really been fortunate enough to have been following him since his start. I would say when he won his first Wimbledon and I remember how much it meant to him. Finally winning the first major and helping him out with the post-match (media obligations). Then I was lucky enough to go on a couple of trips that he did for his Foundation and the ATP followed him as well, to help him with the media and the distribution of video footage and photos and news from there. It's been fantastic to work with him."

Question: Has he changed from his younger days, media-wise?

Nicola Arzani: "Yes he has. I think he's been getting better and better every year. Because he's become more mature, he's really understood his role. He was great at the beginning, but by winning titles, it's not like he's cut down on his commitments but he's continued to improve and develop in that area. I think he likes working with the media. But he likes something different, like a different angle, being challenged about other topics than just tennis or how do you feel about how you played or what do you think about your next opponent type of thing. But I think he also loves the global reach that tennis has and his impact on a lot of countries."

"I remember two things - once in Dubai we had one TV network come down from Pakistan, like a huge network, they came down just to interview him. And I said, Look, we're going to be so busy, I can give you just two questions. Because I have more than ten TVs. They still came just to have Roger for two questions. And same here in Miami, I remember once Globo - they're the biggest TV network in Brazil. They came all the way, with the camerman, the whole crew, to do five minutes with Roger for the evening news back in Brazil. So the interest that he really gets when he arrives everywhere is amazing."

Question: Any funny or unusual requests or memories?

Nicola Arzani: "Those two really stand out - the Brazilians coming here in Miami and the people from Pakistan going to Dubai just for two questions. The agenda was so full. You would remember when Roger and Rafa did the promo for the exhibition matches and they just couldn't make it. It took them, I don't know how long, you can see it on You Tube. They had to do a couple of promos in Cincinnati for the two matches that they played in Madrid and Zurich and they just couldn't do it. Just hilarious. They were together, Rafa missed one line and they started laughing and it went on and on. They couldn't keep a straight face."

"With everything, he cannot absolutely do everything, he cannot attend to all the requests otherwise he would be day and night doing media. But if he commits to do something on the court and off the court, he will do it 100%, even if it's one question, two questions, 20 minutes, half hour, photo shoot, he will do it 100% professionally. He won't do something just for, Okay, I need to do it, fine, I'll do it. But he does it. He gives the best answer, he prepares. He asks a lot of things to people, to make them feel comfortable, not only ask them questions but there's an exchange with them. He's on the same level with the people that interview him. I would say he makes everybody feel extremely at ease and extremely comfortable around them."

Lloyd Carroll (Journalist): "It was in the middle of the second week at the 2012 U.S. Open. I was going down the steps from the second floor of the player lounge area in the Ashe building. And he was climbing the steps. And I just passed him and I said, 'Roger, I enjoyed your Mercedes Benz commercial', the one where the little three-year-old daughter throws the stuffed animal at him. And he seemed really touched by it. He said, 'Really? Did you?' I said, 'Yeah, it actually won a CLEO Award which is like an Academy Award for TV commercials.' It was very well done. He seemed very touched that somebody paid attention to it. It's not the kind of thing that gets talked about during U.S. Open week. I thought he showed kind of a human side, that he actually cared what you thought. But I've always found him a decent guy. You pass him by in the hallway, he'll shake your hand and say hello. He's not - as opposed to the Williams sisters - who probably see right through you. Because I've passed them in the same situation - it always reminds me of the dolphins in Sea World. In other words, when they're on in the press room, they're great. But if you see them outside of it, they'll ignore you totally, they're not on. They're like the dolphins in the pool. The one time Serena actually gave me a nod one time when I passed. That was unusual for her. But Roger will always stop and at least give you a quick hello. If he recognizes you and he knows that you are part of the tennis community."

Jayita Belcourt (Tennis-prose.com): "I have met Roger, years ago as a fan, he signed a calendar for me. I remember when he went to sign my name, he looked at the piece of paper and asked specifically about the "mark" above the "a" and asked if it was part of my name. I said it was and he took the time to write out 'Dear Jayita' with exact precision and signed the paper. I remember thinking what an incredibly detailed, meticulous and caring person he was for someone so busy and accomplished. I also remember when I was doing media coverage at the Australian Open last year and Roger was waiting to play Bernard Tomic. I remember seeing Roger down the bottom - before he comes onto the main court - and wow, he was so incredibely nervous. He was shaking and moving and having to do push-ups to move his 'nervous tension' all about. His face was stressed and he wasn't smiling. And I remember thinking: My God, this tennis 'legend' who has won so many Grand Slams... still gets super freakin' nervous. It was quite fascinating to watch."

Claude Abrams (Former Boxing News Editor): "Federer...has there ever been a greater all around sports figure?"

Richard Pagliaro (Tennis.com Journalist): "I remember a few years back interviewing him one-on-one at the United Nations about 20 minutes before he was going out to speak to the entire United Nations and he was so relaxed. I asked him to sign the Tennis Week cover from when he won his first Wimbledon, the 'Federer Express' cover and he looks at it and smiles and said 'Yeah, I love this cover! This is my favorite one.' I thought that was cool, plus the fact he actually does every press conference in three languages – English, Swiss-German and French, so he actually spends three times more than any other top player talking to the media."

Richard Evans (Tennis Author and Journalist): "Hall of Famer Frew McMillan on BBC Radio and John Parsons in the London Daily Telegraph were two shrewd observers who stuck obstinately to the belief that Federer would ultimately come through, and both tipped him for the title before Wimbledon began. And when he won, Federer was not the only one in tears. McMillan was too. For those of us who have a deep love for this beautiful game, seeing it so beautifully played strikes an emotional chord."

Steve Tignor (Tennis Magazine Columnist and Author): "1999 at Key Biscayne. Roger had like the blond hair highlights. And we did a photo shoot with him out between a couple of trees on the beach. And he was good, he was funny. He had just lost and we were talking about his career and the future for him - he was 17 then. He said, after he lost (to Kenneth Carlsen 5-7 6-7), 'Well, after today, I don't even know if I have a career.'"

John Jeansonne (New York Newsday): "My first memory of Federer...all red outfit, pony-tail, headband. And he could play. I think it was the semifinals at the U.S. Open. And my wife and I went as spectators, I wasn't working that day. And she said, 'Who is this guy?' And I really didn't know. But he could really play. Very smooth. Same as now. Except he didn't win all the time yet."

Gary Swain (IMG Vice President): "I don't remember exactly what year but it was U.S. Open time, New York City. And Roger Federer was hosting a party a couple of days before the start of the U.S. Open. It was at Pasti's, lower Manhattan. And he invited about 50 guests. Everybody arrived. I was one of them and I was amazed, just a few days before he's to play in the tournament - one of the biggest tournaments of the year - he waited the entire evening to say goodbye to every single guest on the way out. I was the very last person to leave - I know that because I and my date were the very last ones to leave with two other people. And he personally greeted every single person on the way out, till about 11 o'clock at night. And it's just one of many examples of the incredible class and business acumen of Roger Federer, as a person beyond maybe the greatest tennis player ever."

Question: Was that the first time you met him?

Gary Swain: "Oh, no. He was a client. I'm with IMG. I've been a Senior Vice President, I've been with the company for 26 years. Up until about a year ago when he left our company, he was a client for many years. I've produced and promoted and staged events that he's participated in. Tony Godsick, who left our company IMG but was his manager, is a good friend of mine. We've toured with John McEnroe, my client, through a number of places. And Roger's the real deal, he's everything you think he is and more. I always remember John saying about Roger - which is probably more important than what I say - that he truly loves what he does and he loves playing tennis and with all the pressures that go with being No. 1 and a world champion, he actually loves every minute of it."

Question: Do you remember your very first memory of Roger?

Gary Swain: "Very first memory...wow. I think my first memory was when I saw him playing at Wimbledon. I don't know what year it was. But he was very young. And people were talking about him. I don't think people were saying - at least not what I was hearing - that he would be the greatest ever, by any means. But they were saying he was gonna be a factor in Grand Slams. I remember seeing him and there was no question about his talent but even at that age I can't say that I would have put any money on him being the greatest ever but you never know. He peaked, I want to say, later...it wasn't like you knew when he was 18 he was gonna be the greatest ever - or even a great champion. You knew he had potential. Then everybody knows what happened after that."

David Mercer (BBC Sport): "My first memory of Roger is commentating on him playing Andre Agassi at the Swiss Indoors in his home town of Basel in 1998. He was only 17 but, although he lost 6-3 6-2, it was quite clear that he was an outstanding young talent. Mind you he also had quite a temper in those days. Since then I must have commentated on hundreds of his matches and it has been a real pleasure to see him develop into, in my opinion, the greatest player of all time and also a fabulous ambassador for tennis."

Jo-Wilfried Tsonga: "We are close like tennis players. We have a good relationship in the locker room. I've got a lot of respect for him. He's just an incredible tennis player. I mean, an example for many people. I have respect for him outside of the court, and on the court I have to - how do you say - disrespect him? Because if you respect him too much, then for sure you lost. So it's different on the court. On the court, I will try to beat him. And I'm sure it's going to be the same thing for him."

Gabriel Markus (Former ATP Player/Coach): "Federer practiced with many of my players when I was with (Nicolas) Massu, (Luis) Horna and (Mikhail) Kukushkin. He was a very, very, very nice guy, very relaxed, good humor. We practiced many times. Always the practices were where he was laughing and relaxing and talking between the games. It was a nice experience. He was, I think, a very good guy to practice."

Question: Standout memory of Federer?

Gabriel Markus: "I remember he was always asking about Argentina. How are the people there, how is the crowd there. And finally he came to Argentina (December 2012) and he had a very good time, full stadium 20,000 for two matches with (Juan Martin) Del Potro."

Question: Lasting memory of Federer?

Gabriel Markus: "Everybody speaks about who is the best in history and, of course, a few say Pete Sampras, a few say him. I think he and Sampras were the best ever. Both were six years like No. 1 ATP. Unbelievably tough. But he had the ability the other ones didn't have - to play and win on every surface. I think he could really be the best in history."

Jay Berger (Former ATP Player and Current USTA Developmental Coach): "It was interesting that I was surprised that he knew who I was, he knows how I served. I've had some of our players hit with him. Actually, he's been unbelievable to the young American players. Last year at the U.S. Open, one of our kids Stefan Kozlov, at 14, hit with Roger. And I was pretty concerned. I was telling Jose Higueras, God, I would love to have Federer hit with him. Paul Annacone is very nice and always calls us about finding hitting partners, young Americans. And I said about Stefan, how could I put a 14-year-old...and Roger was just gracious. He actually asked to hit with him for three or four days. That was really nice."

Question: Any memorable conversation with Roger?

Jay Berger: "Maybe a year ago, and it was interesting. He was very inquisitive and asked a lot of questions about where do you live? Okay, I live in Key Biscayne. What's the life like there? He was very interested, asking a lot of questions. Inquisitive on life, other people's lives, like mine."

Greg Sharko (ATP Director of Media Information): "In Toronto. My family was there visiting the tournament. I introduced them to Roger. So I was going to take a picture with them and him. He said, 'Oh, hold on. Get in the picture.' And had someone else take the picture. So I thought that was very thoughtful. And that's the way his thoughts are - thinking of people."

Peter Haas (Father of Tommy Haas): "I know Roger very well. Tommy trains with him sometimes in Switzerland and other places. I'm a total, big-time Federer fan. Basically speaking, Tommy plays just like Roger, they both have the same old school backhand. That automatically makes me a Federer fan. They basically have the same basic type of game from an aesthetic point of view."

Question: What is your first memory of Roger Federer?

Peter Haas: "It's kind of a funny story. About approximately 12 or 13 years ago down in Miami, South Beach, Ocean Drive. I was walking down the sidewalk. Back then, Tommy wore a bit of a ponytail in the back. So I saw him and said, 'Tommy! Tommy!' This frickin' guy wouldn't turn around. I was thinking: What are you, like deaf?! And it happened to be Roger Federer, who was sitting there with his coach

Peter Lundgren [smiles]."

Question: You've obviously gotten to know Roger, can you share a memory or anecdote that may capture his essence?

Peter Haas: "I know Roger through Tommy. I am very friendly with Mirka. From tennis coaching I know her for ten years before she met Roger at the 2000 Sydney Olympics. I've never seen a tennis player - and I've met many athletes and champions from all professions throughout Tommy's entire career - as a person and a complete athlete, Roger is so friendly, so cordial, so open with people. With zero arrogance. The hair on my arm is almost standing up right now. What I'm saying, in essence, it's almost unbelievable that this type of person exists. He's such a pure, class act. In other words, he's humble. Yet he does not need to be."

Question: Is it hard for your son to play such a close friend like Federer?

Peter Haas: "On the court, they're always going to be fierce competitors. They each have to fight for themselves to win the match. But once the match is over, they're friends. But when it comes to the match they have to be warriors and gladiators. And they accept each other's performance. It's a lot easier for Tommy to accept to lose to Federer, or win, and Federer is the same way if he loses against Tommy. Federer is man enough to say: Hey I lost to Tommy, I lost to a great player. In a nutshell, it's respect."

Peter Holtermann (Holtermann Media): "Two anecdotes. I think it was in 2008, Green Bay was playing the New York Giants in the NFC Championship game. And I have to say, I was wearing my Packers shirt on game day with a little Packer logo on it. And the game was on during the Australian Open. People were watching it in the locker room. James Blake is like a big Giants fan and he saw me after the game to let me know that he was watching in the locker room. So later that day I'm working with ESPN - I gotta get Roger for an interview. So he comes out and he looks at my shirt and he goes, 'Ha, hey why did your guys throw it to the other team at the end?' I don't expect Roger to know anything about football. But there he was, barely knowing about it, but willing to jab about the painful Brett Favre interception. And then, professionaly, we did the BNP Paribas Showdown in New York (in 2012). We have a cocktail reception the night before the event at the Jumeirah Essex House. We have the players come for 30 minutes. And the reception lasts for 90. Roger came in with all the other players. And, literally, the string quartet band was picking up and leaving and Roger was still there talking to people. He was still there, 30 minutes after the party officially ended, talking with people, being generous with his time, you know, the consummate professional."

Brad Falkner (Tennis Channel producer): "It was at Indian Wells in 2004. He'd just beaten Tim Henman. The day before I'd done an interview with Henman and Federer was in the room and he was playfully interrupting. He was talking about wineries because I was asking Tim questions about wine and Tim said he had a wine cellar and Federer was just kind of being cheeky with him and you could tell they were really good buddies. And the ATP actually apologized to me: 'Well, we're sorry Roger kept interrupting your interview with Tim, but they're such good buddies.' So the next day Federer goes out and beats Tim pretty badly and literally, Federer and I are in the same bathroom for some reason. And we're washing our hands. And I look at him in the mirror and said, 'That wasn't very nice what you did to your friend out there.' And he looks at me and smiles, 'Well, he wasn't very nice to me the last few years either.' As you know, at one time Federer had a bad record against Tim Henman."

Charlie Pasarell (Former Indian Wells tournament director): "I remember way back, Gavin Forbes (player agent) from IMG said there's this young Swiss kid Roger Federer, he plays the game like it should be played, and he plays like Sampras. And, of course, I heard of him, I knew he was a pretty good junior and everything. And I was looking for a wildcard in Indian Wells. And I said, 'Sure, we'll give it to him.' And needless to say, the guy turned out to be maybe the greatest of all time. At least, when you talk about the greatest of all time, Roger Federer's name will have to come up, way up at the top."

"He's just a remarkable player. He is so effortless in how he plays the game. I actually call him the Nureyev of the tennis court. He floats. He doesn't really run, he just floats out there. It's a God-given talent. He has a great temperment for his sport. And he plays the game, no excuses. Like in (Indian Wells 2013), his back was bothering him. He still played and he had no excuses. And that's the way he is. He is truly one of the great champions of all times, not just because of the titles he won but how he approaches the game with such class and such style. He's a real credit to the game. We love to have him."

Question: Can you share an example of any personal interaction you have had with Federer?

Charlie Pasarell: "He and I have a very cordial relationship. As a past tournament director, I would try to stay out of the player's way. I always just wanted to make sure that when they came to Indian Wells that they were comfortable, that if they needed something, they shouldn't hesitate to ask. I think the last sort of interchange I had with him was last year (2012). When he arrived at Indian Wells, he said his entire family was very sick. And they were renting a house. The two girls were sick and the nanny was sick and everybody was sick. And so I said, 'Have you seen a doctor?' (Roger replied) 'No.' 'I'll arrange things. I'll have a doctor there within an hour.' And so, sure enough, we sent a doctor. He was there within a half an hour. He took care of the families. So that's kind of how I deal with the players. I just try to pretty much stay out of the way, make sure they feel that they can always come to me and ask for something and I'll do my utmost to deliver it. And I like it that way."

Chapter 10 Memorable Federer Quotes:

When the champion speaks, the world listens...

* "Maybe people haven't seen a guy play like I have and that gives me a lot of compliments. That's beautiful."

* "I'm so happy the way things are going, I'm so proud of all my results and the way I kind of handled things. It's tough but it's a great life and I wouldn't exchange it for anything."

* "I hope I'm remembered as one of the good guys, fair, kind of an idol to the kids. Because that's what I needed to get started."

* "It's not so much the pressure of being No. 1, it's more the time, you have less time. Everybody wants to talk with you, ask you questions. There's always something going on, something to do. Once I'm on the court, that's not so much the pressure, that's the easy part. It's what I love to do."

* On playing Tim Henman: "He's beaten me six times. I've beaten him twice. His game has given me difficulties in the past."

* On Marcelo Rios in 2006: "I think he could play both Tours (ATP and Seniors), he's that good. I'm happy to see him play at all, you know, because of all the injuries he's had, good career he's had. It would be a disappointment not to see him play at all. He's such a unique player with a lot of talent. I would love to see him back on Tour. You know, that's where I would like to see him. Not the Senior's Tour."

* On his early career doubts and dislikes about playing certain players: "I think Nalbandian a little bit in the beginning. Henman and Hewitt. I think early on in your career it's more extreme than later on - for me anyway - just because when I got to No. 1 I sort of beat everybody. Before that my game wasn't as good as today (2009). I didn't have that many options. I realized against Nalbandian I was panicking. I had to run to the net to try to force the envelope. Against Hewitt, it was sort of similar. Every time I would come to net, he would pass or

lob me. It was just really tough. Henman was just uncomfortable because he was always coming at me. In the beginning, my returns weren't good enough, my mental, my fitness. It was good but it wasn't great yet. And that's why those were matches I didn't like to play. So I was happy I could actually turn many of those win-loss records around. They all had unique playing styles. It was interesting playing them."

* "I've had many people you look up to - come to you and say, 'I'm your biggest fan!' And you say, 'Really? You?' That happens occasionally, and it's funny."

* "The first junior match I ever played, I lost 6-0 6-0 to Reto Schmidli."

* "One good thing about me is that I forget matches, even bad matches, very quickly. I get sad about not having played well but I don't really get upset. By the time I get back to the hotel, it's completely forgotten and I'm fine."

* At a U.S. Open press conference I asked Roger if there was a secret to his success? "I guess not, no. Hard work and belief that I can win every match I play. I've come a long way. I never thought I'll ever play so well and dominate tennis. I'm just really having a great time."

* "I just like to watch tennis. If I'm flipping through the channels and see a match – really no matter who is playing – I just like the game very much. One player I would really like to watch is Bjorn Borg because I never really had the chance to see him when he was at his best. And from what I've seen and heard, he is a very special player. And obviously a great champion."

* "I used to carry on like an idiot, I was getting kicked out of practice sessions non-stop when I was 16. Then after winning junior Wimbledon (in '98) people were coming up to me and telling me I was going to be the next great player. But at first I wasn't mentally strong enough and I found myself getting frustrated when things didn't go my way."

* "I remember this moment when I was playing Safin in Rome one time, and they were showing highlights after the match and sort of trying to say who was better in throwing racquets. And then I really started to realize this is not why I'm playing tennis, to be in a competition of who's throwing the racquet more nicely [smiles]."

* I asked Roger at the 2008 U.S. Open this question: What's been the greatest comeback in your career? And the opposite, the worst-blown lead in your career?

"The worst-blown lead, maybe Davis Cup against Lleyton 2003 in the semifinals, serving for the match, two points from it, two sets to love. But. My best one, I don't know. Maybe Rafa in Miami. I was down two sets to love and came back and won. So I guess that."

* On his friendship with Tim Henman: "I think the way he goes at work, I never had a bad practice with Tim. They've all been good. He's always so into it, but with the fun side next to it. Always very sportsmanship-like on the tennis court during matches. Yeah, I always enjoyed playing against him, spending time with him. Of course, he was older, so I always looked up to him, as well."

* On Patty Schnyder: "She was the first from the region of Basel who made the breakthrough. I saw her beat the best in the world. She was an inspiration for me. I remember especially her brother Danny. He's a good friend and we often played against each other. Patty was older. Girls develop even earlier. I always looked up to her. I ballboyed for her at a tournament in Basel. I followed her career closely. Patty was always very nice to me. I also to her, I think. And she also got along well with Mirka, who she played."

* "My inspiration is the new generation, the pack chasing me. The possible chance of rewriting history, if possible. Then, for myself. So I have three different sources of inspiration."

* "I made the breakthrough early, but for years I've always looked at the long-term. I think that helps me to play for a long period of time, hopefully. It was always my goal to play until 35 or more. For that reason, I still feel I have many more years to go."

* "He (John McEnroe) was an amazing player and brought a lot to the game, like some other great champions and legends have done and paved the way for us. We can only be thankful for everything he gave to tennis, because he didn't just stop after he stopped playing. He kept commentating and kept the game exciting for fans and TV and so forth and even plays seniors still a lot and keeps on promoting tennis."

* On the differences between night matches at the Australian Open and U.S. Open...

"Well, I guess obviously the center court is a bit different because the U.S. Open comes closer to the player. The Australian Open, everything is further up, all the way around. Here on the sides, it comes closer, so automatically you're more in contact with the fans. The stadium is bigger. Depending on who plays here, it can be very, very loud, you know. Always something happening on change of ends. You have the music, then you have, you know there's always something going on, where at the Australian Open it's much more focused on maybe just alone on the players."

"They have a roof over there, so I guess there the atmosphere stays more within the court. Here, it goes more out, obviously. So similar, but so different. You got to talk to more players to try to get information, I think."

----
* On feeling sorry for blowing out an opponent (2006 U.S. Open)...

121

Q. Last night Andre Agassi said when he has a match as easy as his was and as easy as yours was today, he doesn't feel sorry for his opponent. Do you?

Roger Federer: No, I don't. I used to. That was a problem for me. Like I had the feeling the guy deserves it more than I do. That's a horrible feeling to have inside. Especially when I was playing juniors or coming on Tour. No, that feeling is definitely gone. That's good.

Q. Why do you think the guy deserved it more than you?

Roger Federer: I don't know. Because I had the feeling maybe they were practicing harder than I was. I was lucky enough to be in Switzerland, you know how it is. Couldn't get over it sometimes.

Q. How did you lose that feeling of guilt or whatever it was?

Roger Federer: Well, it's just the fire to win, always wanting to be the best. I think once you get that going, then you realize, you know, if you lose or win, you can still chat after the match. But then when I would lose matches, I would feel I think three times worse than when the guy was losing. I just realized that's not the point either. I wanted to enjoy it, win or lose, out on the court. It's not some kind of war or anything. We're having fun out there in the end. I like the challenge. When the match is over, you know, life goes on.

----

* On James Blake: "I think he's very flashy on the court. He's an incredible shot-maker. One of the best we have in the game. Off the court, he's a nice guy. Nice to hang out with."

* On looking back eight years in 2012, becoming No. 1 the first time in 2004: "I do remember it very vividly, actually. It's not one of those moments that happens and then you forget. It took me a lot of great performances to get there. I had an opportunity I think in the match against Roddick in Montréal. Lost 7-6 in the semis there against him. It took me to win Wimbledon, the World Tour Finals, then basically get to the finals of the Australian Open. After beating Ferrero in the semis, I knew I clinched it, but obviously I wanted to finish the tournament on a high note winning the Australian Open as well."

"That's what I was able to do then. But I remember after the semis how happy I was becoming World No. 1. It was for me back then sort of the ultimate accomplishment next to winning Wimbledon. That all happened in a span of sort of nine months, which was so intense, huge relief in some ways, but a big satisfaction. Here I am eight years later, even more. It's pretty special. Obviously I lost the World No. 1 ranking a few times, but I also stayed a long time once I got there. I always felt tennis was easier for me playing as World No. 1 than actually getting there."

* Federer expressed that he still simply loves to play the game of tennis, not

necessarily just winning... "Sometimes you're just happy playing. Some people, some media unfortunately don't understand that it's okay just to play tennis and enjoy it. They always think you have to win everything, it always needs to be a success story, and if it's not obviously what is the point? Maybe you have to go back and think, *Why have I started playing tennis?* Because I just like it. It's actually sort of a dream hobby that became somewhat of a job. Some people just don't get that ever."

----

* Federer quotes after losing 2012 London Barclays ATP World Tour Finals to Djokovic...

"I think it's the love for the game, the appreciation I get from the crowds, I guess playing for records from time to time, playing against different types of generations and playing styles. The game has evolved sort of over the last 13-14 years I've been on Tour. It's changed quite a bit ever since."

"I think you need inspiration, motivation from different angles to keep you going because it isn't that simple just to wake up every morning and go for another travel around the world, another practice, all these other things, another fitness workout, another stretch. It's always nice, but you need to have some success and you need to have the right reasons why you're doing it. I think I've always been able to do that and I really enjoy myself out on the court."

"Today was no different. Doesn't mean it's not fun when you lose - it's definitely not nice - but it also can be entertaining and fun for me if I play a match like today."

"It's part of the puzzle that makes me motivated, trying to play against them, but Novak, Andy and Rafa are not the only guys out there. I'm trying to play against many other guys. I love playing against particularly young guys as well just because, to many, sometimes I'm an idol, which is very strange to me, to be honest. But it's nice seeing them grow, see what the next generation comes up with, what kind of playing style. So for me, that would suffice, as well. Then, of course, unfortunately you have guys retiring now that are my age. That's been fun, too, still seeing them playing as well, like Tommy Haas, [Andy] Roddick, [Lleyton] Hewitt, [Juan Carlos] Ferrero."

"I think it's been a fantastic season to be part of. Four different Grand Slam champs. Then having the Olympics, as well, was obviously very unique. I'm very happy I stayed injury free throughout. That allowed me to basically play a full schedule almost. I'm very pleased that I was able to pick up my performance at the end of the season, like I played now this week, so obviously gives me confidence for next year."

Chapter 11: Coach Perspectives On Federer

Various ATP coaches share insights and memories of their encounters of facing Roger Federer in ATP professional matches...

Brian Barker (Former coach of James Blake): "Federer played some unbelievable matches against James. They played in the finals of Indian Wells. The level that Federer played was just off the charts. And he was just overwhelming with his forehand and backhand. And also James played him in the finals of Shanghai. It was one of those days where Federer was hitting, obviously his forehand, extremely explosive and big. He was also hitting his backhand with that kind of force. And moving James all over the court."

"Those two matches stick out in my mind. I remember saying to James after he played him in Shanghai - James was like, What was I supposed to do when he plays like that? - I don't know if there's much you can do. And Federer said after, that it was 'one of the better matches I played.' When he plays like that - possibly the best player that ever played - playing his best tennis, is kind of tough."

Question: What was the strategy to beat Federer at the Athens Olympics in 2004? What happened there?

Barker: "Well, James' strategy against most players, including Federer, is to move people and for James to try to get a lot of forehands himself. To try to play aggressive, not make it into a touch match or a finesse match. On that day James was was just really on top of his game, seeing the ball as big as he ever has. And Federer, for sure, was a little bit off that day. Not playing quite his best. James kept rushing him, so it just went his way for the two sets."

Question: What do you think were the greatest performances of James' career, the best matches he ever played?

Barker: "I think at Shanghai when James made the top 6 in 2006, he played Nadal first round in round robin and beat him in straight sets. That was one of the best matches that he'd ever played. He beat Nadal two times before that. Once at the U.S. Open and played really well. Then at Indian Wells, the semis, he played really well. Nadal came out guns blazing that match and James played absolutely his best tennis to fend him off in straight sets. Then probably the semis of Shanghai that year when he played Nalbandian. And he won in pretty convincing manner, in straight sets. Those were two of the better matches James ever played."

Question: Did you ever have any personal interaction with Federer through the years?

Barker: "James would practice with him, so yeah, certainly here and there, just talk to him and say hello. And shootin' the breeze. One conversation with Federer, when he was just a young kid, not ranked very high in the world. And we were in Indianapolis. I remember we were watching golf on TV. And he was saying how lucky these pro golfers are, they go to beautiful places, they get to do something that they love. And they get to make money doing something they love. In some of the nicest places in the world. And he said, 'These guys are just so lucky.' And to myself I was thinking: 'Yeah, you're lucky.'"

"And then two minutes later he looked at me and said, 'You know what? It's like kind of like us. Like, we're so lucky. We have this perfect life where we get to do what we love to do, in these great places. And we're really lucky (with) this life that we have.' I remember thinking: This is just such a nice kid with a good perspective. And a good head on his shoulders. And he just understands life and how lucky he is. How his life fits in with everything else. I just remember thinking this kid's gonna do really well. And he's gonna be happy with whatever he does, whatever it is. And he has just such a great attitude."

Bob Brett (Coach of Marin Cilic, Mario Ancic and Goran Ivanisevic): "Federer has set a standard for movement in the game and what opportunities exist during a point. That for me was the most impressive part. And I would go back to one of the best matches I ever saw him play was the match against Ferrer in Shanghai, maybe 2006, 2007. And it was just very impressive how he got inside the court. Really was a great example of what can be done."

Question: What is your first memory of Roger Federer?

Bob Brett: "That's a long time ago! I remember him...I knew Peter Carter who was coaching him. He was traveling with Peter sometimes on the Tour. When you saw him the first time you knew he was going to be a good player."

Question: Some players have said they were not overly impressed by Roger the first time they saw him, such as Andre Agassi and Attila Savolt. Savolt and Peter Luczak said Nalbandian was tougher for them to play.

Bob Brett: "Nalbandian gave him trouble. A player of that type is different. Being able to do a lot of different things, to be able to go to the net, serve and volley, that takes longer to form than it does somebody from the baseline. It's two different games and this one takes longer to mature, whereas look at a lot of people who played from the baseline, they were early maturers. That, I find, is the difference. When someone is playing like that, with that flair, it's going to depend on their commitment, their mind. He really blossomed. It took a while for him to absolutely dominate. And against right-handers, definitely the dominating player, totally, in almost history. Though he had problems and difficulty with Rafa. It's been interesting to watch Federer play tennis and what he could do. A great example for players, coaches and spectators."

Question: How has it been for you trying to coach your players against him?

Bob Brett: "Well, I don't coach against anybody. I remember when I coached Ancic when they played at Wimbledon. And Mario won. And the year before Roger had beaten Sampras and lost in the quarterfinals that year. That match with Sampras surprised everybody. That was the one that shocked. I think Pete wasn't even ready for that. And then the next year it was of course the first match on center court. The grass was a little slippery and Mario won."

Question: Do you remember the tactics that worked so successfully that day against Roger?

Bob Brett: "First of all, Mario did come through qualifying. And that was the thing I thought would be nice to play a top player on center court. And then the rest is personal [laughs]."

Question: Mario must have been playing 'lights out' tennis going into that match?

Bob Brett: "Yeah, of course. He played three matches already in the qualifying. It caught Roger a little by surprise. I don't think he lost to Mario ever again. But that's just part of it. It was one of those things where you have somebody come through qualifying, he's a good player, he's going to be a good player, and surprise. And that's what happened that day. Mario played well. But I think Roger was a little bit more aware, ready. And you can see on that first day, it's not that easy, on the grass at that particular time."

Question: Lasting memory of Roger, on or off court?

Bob Brett: "His example for play. His ability. As his many matches with Nadal have shown, he's been great for tennis worldwide."

Boris Sobkin (Coach of Mikhail Youzhny, who was 0-14 vs. Federer at time time of this interview in 2013): "The first time I met Roger we played the European Team Championships. I think it was under 16. We played in Belgium near the border of Luxembourg. Roger was 16, Mischa was 15 when I saw him the first time. Honestly, he played good for sure. To be honest, I didn't see the genius at the time [smiles]. Maybe I had bad eyes [smiles]. He played really good, it was pretty understandable that he was a good player and a professional player, that was no discussion. But to become so good, I did not expect."

Question: Do you remember who won this match?

Boris Sobkin: "Roger played - I was team captain - Roger played number one. Mischa was actually a substitute on the team. Mischa was 15 at the time, he was no. 3 on the team. The No. 1 on our team - the guy is not playing professionally and no. 2 was Igor Kunitsyn. So Roger played against Igor Sosolev. It was a three sets match actually and Roger won. As far as I remember, we lost the match 2-1."

Question: How do you think Federer has been able to become what he is today, maybe the greatest player in history?

Boris Sobkin: "First of all, first of all, of course, of course he's talented. He's huge talent. If we say 1-2-3 across the board, I say unbelievable head. Everybody talks about his hands, to keep control of the ball at such speed. I think first is his head because he is really smart. He's really smart. He has really special qualities, especially in his hands, arm, shoulders, all this. It's very fast from one side and from the other side he can control the ball. That's very important. Of course, also very good at anticipation. He knows where the ball is going. I think only comparable to him is Andy Murray in anticipation. Roger moves very fast to the hit point. And of course he has good legs and everything is fine. And he's playing so good and so long and probably he's playing more. Compared to others he expends very little energy when he's playing. He's not running so much, he's finishing the point early. He's attacking the ball when it's possible. But he's patient, he can keep the ball in play when it's necessary. So he does everything to be the greatest player. And he is the greatest player now, honestly. I have big respect for the other guys - Nadal or Djokovic or Murray or Ferrer - but I think Roger spends the lowest energy when he's playing. That's why he prevents his body from injuries. From one side, from the other side, it's not tough for him to play every point 20 strokes. It's easy for his head."

Question: Has Mikhail ever beaten Federer?

Boris Sobkin: "No [laughs]. Just once in doubles at junior U.S. Open in doubles. I think it was the year 1998. Roger played doubles with Olivier Rochus. And Mischa played doubles with Karol Beck of Slovakia. And Roger and Rochus won easy first set 6-1 and were up a break in the second and started to make jokes and finally Mischa and Karol beat them. So it was only once unfortunately [laughs]."

Question: What are the tactics for Mischa when he has to play Roger in singles?

Boris Sobkin: "I would say I don't want to discuss this, sorry. Hopefully we will play one or two more matches and Mischa hopefully will one time win."

Question: What's the closest Mischa has come to beating Roger?

Boris Sobkin: "The closest was in Halle, they played on grass. Mischa won the first set, it was 4-3 in tiebreak for Mischa. Roger was serving and Roger went to the net but the ball was on the half court, very close. Mischa can easily put the ball to Roger's body and win the point. But he had respect, he didn't do this. He tried to pass but it's really tough to pass Roger. To the body it was easier. Even if you put easier ball to the body, Roger has no chance. It was really close. But Mischa, being of big respect for Roger, he tried to pass him down the line and Roger reached it and won this point and next point in tiebreak, won the tiebreak and won third set. But it was really close. Because the score becomes 5-3. Mischa played good at this time and he has a really good chance."

Question: When was this match?

Boris Sobkin: "2003 or 2004."

Question: Can you share a lasting memory of Federer? When you think of Roger, what comes to mind?

Boris Sobkin: "He's a really smart person. Really well-educated person. He's the person I like to talk with. It's interesting to talk with him. Honestly, I don't support everything he thinks about tennis, how it should go, about ATP, we have a lot of discussion with him about this. I'm not 100% supporting what he's thinking about this. But I have great respect for him. He's really a great person for tennis, not only a player, I mean in general. Because everybody in the locker room has respect for him. Everybody listen to him. And I really like his family, his wife, I know his wife since she was 16. Long story, it's another story for another book [smiles]. But I really like the family. I have good relations with his father and his mother, they're really nice people. It's really clear why he's so educated. He has really nice family. And he was well educated in the family first. This is very important."

(Note: Youzhny played Federer in the final of Halle in 2013 and before the match stated to the media: "I never beat (Federer). But a new match is a new match. We have the same chances. I don't think that I lost to him 14 times before and I never beat him and I don't have any chances. Nobody knows what happens tomorrow."

(Federer once again defeated Youzhny for the 15th time in the 2013 Halle final 6-7 6-3 6-4.)

Nick Bollettieri: "Federer represents life, he represents family, he represents the sport. Only a few people can do that. He went through some up and down times when he was a youngster. But he learned by those failures. And we shouldn't call them failures. People who don't fail will never reach their ultimate existence. So many people think that failure is the end of the world. No, failure is part of learning. Come back and do it a little differently. Roger Federer, in my opinion, is not only a genius on the court but a genius in how he handles everything. I'm proud that my Paul Annacone, who was with me from 14-years-old and went on to Tennessee, he was one of my star pupils. And only a guy like Paul can relate to a guy like Federer. You need a laid-back guy because Federer is laid-back. And I believe Federer will go down as one of the greatest players in the history of the game."

"He does things without trying. He reminds me of Muhammad Ali how he just dances gracefully. Everything he does, he does without any effort, only a few could do. Number two, he has every shot in the game. Now if I had had Roger as a youngster, with his footwork, I probably would have had him do a two-handed backhand. Especially in these times. Now, back in the 70's and 80's when not too much time was spent on physical fitness, or they went by the gym and said hello [smiles]. The diets are different today. The technology, the racquets and the strings. But, today, overall, and my Tommy Haas has one of the best backhands in the world. (Nicolas) Almagro has a great backhand. (Stan) Wawrinka has a great backhand. And so does Federer. But overall, overall with the speed that Federer had - because the element of reach sometimes with two hands, it limits you somewhat - I think he would have been unbeatable. Because what he did - he also attacked. So staying back is different. But he created and I think he could have, perhaps, done more with a two-handed backhand. However, in the last year or so, Roger became much looser on the backhand. And he's developing more racquet head speed, catching the ball earlier. He's got one of the most beautiful slices in the history of the game. But overall, I wonder sometimes if that guy had a two-handed backhand."

Question: His game might not have been as elegant and artistic though.

Nick Bollettieri: "That's exactly right. That's exactly right. But you know, when you look at the results, you don't look at how elegant he was. If you look at Brad Gilbert - where I wore three pairs of Oakley glasses - sunvabitch was so ugly with his strokes [smiles], but he knew how to win. And he's a great friend of mine. So it may not have been so elegant looking but I believe, overall, in today's game, the two-handed backhand would have been better. Because if you go back two or three or four years ago, how did Nadal beat Federer? Heavy forehand cross courts. Heavy forehand cross courts. Heavy forehand cross courts. And eventually, the longer the match goes on, it's tough. But Roger represents life. He represents family, he represents the sport. He's a gentleman and a genius."

Question: Do you remember the first time you ever met Roger?

Nick Bollettieri: "A long time ago. I never really got to close to him. Tony Godsick became his manager and I always send him a nice e-mail in a text. Always a gentleman, always says hello. But he's the type of guy you don't want to try to impress on who you are. A nice hello, how are you, you're doing great for the game. And walk away."

Match Points

Mikael Pernfors: "I met him a little bit when he was coached by Peter Lundgren. That was before he really got big. I was very impressed with him as a person. I thought he had both feet on the ground and had a really big game that could do really well. Then it did. I think the thing about Roger - not knowing him really well - what I feel is that, a good example for me, is when I go and play the seniors at the French Open every year, whether he's in the locker room and he's gonna go take a shower before he's going out to play the semifinal at the French Open, he'll always come up to you and say hello and ask you how you're doing.

And he learned quite a bit of Swedish with Peter Lundgren. He always comes up and gives you a couple of lines In Swedish. And, I mean, I think it's kind of fun that I know he does it with all the guys, anybody in that locker room. So I think it's a great thing that he has in the sense that he's a great sportsman. But he also understands why he's there. He really has a good attitude how he goes about things. I'm very impressed by him."

Vijay Amritraj: "My first memory of Roger Federer was him beating Pete Sampras at Wimbledon. I was doing television. That was my first real look at him. My impressions were that he was the modern version of the old tennis player. That's all he was. He was just so graceful, he was perfect. He was a great guy to watch playing. He was gonna add a new dimension to the sport. Because of all the other guys coming along...it was great to have someone like that come along."

Question: Do you have any personal memories or interactions with Federer?

Vijay Amritraj: "Well, we're both ambassadors for Rolex. And so we get to do a lot of stuff for them. And recently I did an in-depth interview with him in Dubai (2012) on television which was interesting. And he's a great guy. You know, he's easy, he's charming. And on court he's got the heart of a lion and he's very graceful to watch. He has a great family, his parents are wonderful and he has been a real great asset for the game."

Todd Martin: "I played Federer before he became Federer. We played in Davis Cup in 2001. But, you know, he was special, he hit two of the most amazing shots to me that I've faced in a row in the second set tiebreak. I was down a set. I played a couple of very good attacking points in that tiebreak. He hit a running forehand lob winner. And then a running backhand topspin lob winner. And the forehand lob was great, the backhand lob was ridiculous. And so that was like, geez, you know, that's different. There are not many guys who responded to my best tennis and he came up with stuff that I couldn't respond to at all."

"And then the other thing I remember from playing him was - he uses the short slice a lot. And I felt like it was a nothing shot. But at the same time I wasn't able to do anything against it. It was not like Todd Woodbridge and some other guys used that shot a lot, but it really put me in an awkward position. And with Roger, he'd sort of junk it short. And it was like nothing really - I'm gonna pass you if you come in, I'm gonna hurt you if you stay back. Even though it was not, in a vacuum, a great shot."

Question: Do you have any lasting memories of Roger on or off court, that maybe captures his essence?

Todd Martin: "The greatest amount of memories that I have of Roger were when I wasn't playing. And how dominant he was. The match when he beat Hewitt 0, six, and 0 at the U.S. Open. It looked like it should be 0 and 0. It just had that feel. He was just so dominant. But also - and this is what I like most about him - is that every moment of his career, he makes it look like he's out there playing a game. It doesn't look like he's playing something of greater importance than a tennis match. And yet he competes like an absolute dog, he fights so hard without showing that he's fighting so hard. And as graceful as he is around the courts, he's a more graceful person and competitor."

Question: Any memorable interaction with him? How do you get along with Roger?

Todd Martin: "Oh yeah, I don't know anybody who doesn't get along with him. He's as easy as can be."

Note: Very special thanks to photo contributions by Andy Kentla, Henk Abbink, Ziggy, Wojciech Kubik (cover photo). Also special thanks to artwork contributions by Stephen Burkett, Gaspar Geza (Federer sculpture), John Murawski (Federer oil painting), and Andres Bella ("Who Framed Roger Federer" artwork).

About the Author.

Mark "Scoop" Malinowski first started covering professional tennis in 1992 at the Pathmark Classic exhibition in Mahwah, N.J. He has written about tennis and Biofiled players for such media outlets as Tennis Magazine, Tennis Week Magazine, Tennis Magazine Australia, Ace Magazine (U.K.), www.ATPWorldTour.com, New York Tennis, Florida Tennis, Totally Tennis, Tennis View Magazine, among other outlets. He founded the web site www.Tennis-prose.com in 2011

Scoop has Biofile interviewed Don Budge, Jack Kramer, Roger Federer, Pete Sampras, Ivan Lendl, Chris Evert, Billie Jean King, Tracy Austin, Manuel Santana, Novak Djokovic, Rafael Nadal, Bud Collins, Stefan Edberg, Mats Wilander, Guillermo Vilas, among hundreds of other. His first book about tennis was "Marcelo Rios: The Man We Barely Knew."

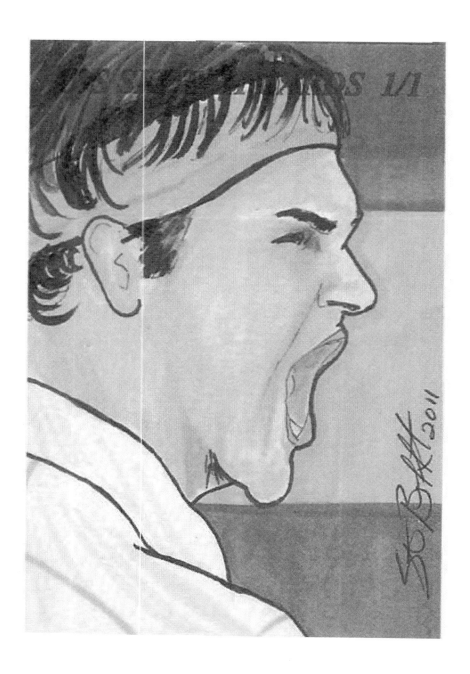

Made in the USA
Lexington, KY
04 November 2013